COCKTAILS 2011

FOOD&**WINE**

AMERICAN EXPRESS PUBLISHING CORPORATION, NEW YORK

FOOD & WINE COCKTAILS 2011

EDITOR **Kate Krader**
DEPUTY EDITOR **Jim Meehan**
SENIOR EDITOR **Colleen McKinney**
ASSISTANT EDITOR/TESTER **Lindsay Nader**
COPY EDITOR **Lisa Leventer**
RESEARCHER **Jill Benz Malter**
EDITORIAL ASSISTANT **Sonam Hajela**
RECIPE INTERN **Maggie Mariolis**
RESEARCH INTERN **Angela McKee**

ART DIRECTOR **Courtney Waddell Eckersley**
DESIGNER **Noah Cornell**
PRODUCTION MANAGER **Matt Carson**
FOOD RECIPE TESTERS **Grace Parisi,
Marcia Kiesel, Justin Chapple**

PHOTOGRAPHER **Tina Rupp**
FOOD STYLIST **Alison Attenborough**
PROP STYLIST **Michelle Wong**

ON THE COVER **(left) Bargoens Buck, P. 136; (center)
Platinum Sparkle, P. 30; The Don's Bramble, P. 110**

AMERICAN EXPRESS PUBLISHING CORPORATION

PRESIDENT/C.E.O. **Ed Kelly**
CHIEF MARKETING OFFICER & PRESIDENT, DIGITAL
MEDIA **Mark V. Stanich**
S.V.P./CHIEF FINANCIAL OFFICER **Paul B. Francis**
V.P.S/GENERAL MANAGERS **Frank Bland,
Keith Strohmeier**

V.P., BOOKS & PRODUCTS/PUBLISHER
Marshall Corey
DIRECTOR, BOOK PROGRAMS **Bruce Spanier**
SENIOR MARKETING MANAGER, BRANDED BOOKS
Eric Lucie
ASSISTANT MARKETING MANAGER **Stacy Mallis**
DIRECTOR OF FULFILLMENT & PREMIUM VALUE
Phil Black
MANAGER OF CUSTOMER EXPERIENCE &
PRODUCT DEVELOPMENT **Charles Graver**
DIRECTOR OF FINANCE **Thomas Noonan**
ASSOCIATE BUSINESS MANAGER **Uma Mahabir**
OPERATIONS DIRECTOR (PREPRESS)
Rosalie Abatemarco Samat
OPERATIONS DIRECTOR (MANUFACTURING)
Anthony White

ISBN 978-1-60320-882-6
ISSN 1554-4354

FOOD & WINE MAGAZINE

S.V.P./EDITOR IN CHIEF **Dana Cowin**
CREATIVE DIRECTOR **Stephen Scoble**
MANAGING EDITOR **Mary Ellen Ward**
EXECUTIVE EDITOR **Pamela Kaufman**
EXECUTIVE FOOD EDITOR **Tina Ujlaki**
EXECUTIVE WINE EDITOR **Ray Isle**
EXECUTIVE DIGITAL EDITOR **Rebecca Bauer**
DEPUTY EDITOR **Christine Quinlan**

FEATURES
RESTAURANT EDITOR **Kate Krader**
TRAVEL EDITOR **Jen Murphy**
STYLE EDITOR **Jessica Romm**
ASSOCIATE WINE EDITOR **Megan Krigbaum**
ASSISTANT EDITORS **Alessandra Bulow,
Kelly Snowden**
EDITORIAL ASSISTANT **Soomin Shon**

FOOD
DEPUTY EDITOR **Kate Heddings**
ASSOCIATE EDITORS **Kristin Donnelly,
Daniel Gritzer**
TEST KITCHEN SUPERVISOR **Marcia Kiesel**
SENIOR RECIPE DEVELOPER **Grace Parisi**
ASSISTANT RECIPE TESTER **Justin Chapple**

ART
ART DIRECTOR **Courtney Waddell Eckersley**
SENIOR DESIGNER **Michael Patti**
DESIGNER **James Maikowski**

PHOTO
DIRECTOR OF PHOTOGRAPHY **Fredrika Stjärne**
DEPUTY PHOTO EDITOR **Anthony LaSala**
ASSOCIATE PHOTO EDITOR **Sara Parks**
PHOTO ASSISTANT **Vanessa Mack**

PRODUCTION
PRODUCTION MANAGER **Matt Carson**
DESIGN/PRODUCTION ASSISTANT **Carl Hesler**

COPY & RESEARCH
COPY CHIEF **Michele Berkover Petry**
SENIOR COPY EDITOR **Ann Lien**
ASSISTANT RESEARCH EDITORS **Erin Laverty,
John Mantia**

DIGITAL MEDIA
DESIGN DIRECTOR **Patricia Sanchez**
DEPUTY EDITOR **Tracy Ziemer**
ASSOCIATE EDITOR **Lawrence Marcus**
DESIGNER **Jinny Kim**
EDITORIAL PROJECT COORDINATOR **Kerianne Hansen**

Published by
American Express Publishing Corporation
1120 Avenue of the Americas, New York, NY 10036

Manufactured in the United States of America

COCKTAILS
2011

FOOD&**WINE**
BOOKS

CONTENTS

Marasca Acida, P. 106, and Shrimp a la Plancha with Pimentón & Garlic Oil, P. 188

"Patrician" Champagne coupe by Josef Hoffmann for Lobmeyr from Neue Galerie.

s there an excellent restaurant in America that hasn't been caught up in the cocktail revolution? We don't think so. You might even see the chef hanging out behind the bar with the mixologist, shaker in hand. At Atlanta's Restaurant Eugene, for instance, chef-owner Linton Hopkins comes up with enticing drinks like the sidecar-inspired DCV (p. 154); it's one of the great recipes in our brand-new Chefs' Cocktails chapter. Mixologists are thinking more like chefs, too, balancing flavors in ever more sophisticated ways. They might, for example, add a pinch of salt to an herbal drink like the Silver Monk (p. 68). For their help in keeping us on top of these trends, we'd like to thank deputy editor Jim Meehan, who rounded up all the drink recipes in this book, and Lindsay Nader, who tested them. And thanks to the FOOD & WINE Test Kitchen cooks, who tested the amazing party-food recipes, including what might be the world's best snack, Thrice-Cooked Fries (p. 186), courtesy of chef April Bloomfield.

DANA COWIN
EDITOR IN CHIEF
FOOD & WINE MAGAZINE

KATE KRADER
EDITOR
FOOD & WINE COCKTAILS 2011

Colorado Cooler, P. 94

"Equinoxe" highball glass by Baccarat; "Hôtel Silver"
cocktail shaker from Bergdorf Goodman.

COCKTAIL CLINIC

GLASSWARE ARSENAL

1 2 3 4 5 6

1 COLLINS
A very tall, narrow glass often used for drinks served on ice and topped with soda.

2 COUPE
A shallow, wide-mouthed glass primarily for small (short) and potent cocktails.

3 FIZZ
A narrow glass for soda-topped drinks without ice. Also called a Delmonico or juice glass.

4 FLUTE
A tall, slender, usually stemmed glass; its narrow shape helps keep cocktails topped with Champagne or sparkling wine effervescent.

5 HIGHBALL
A tall, narrow glass that helps preserve the fizz in drinks served with ice and topped with club soda or tonic water.

6 MARTINI
A stemmed glass with a cone-shaped bowl for cocktails that are served straight up (drinks that are chilled with ice before they're strained).

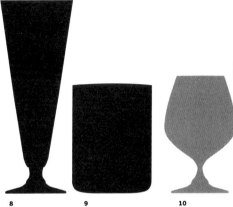

7

8   9   10   11

7 PINT
A large, flared
16-ounce glass,
ideally made of
tempered glass,
used for stirring
drinks or for
serving oversize
cocktails with
generous
amounts of ice.

8 PILSNER
A flared glass
designed for beer.
It's also good for
serving oversize
cocktails or drinks
with multiple
garnishes.

9 DOUBLE ROCKS
A short, wide-
mouthed glass for
spirits served
neat and cocktails
poured over ice.
SINGLE ROCKS
glasses hold
around 6 ounces;
double rocks
hold closer to 12.

10 SNIFTER
A wide-bowled
glass for warm
drinks, cocktails
on ice and spirits
served neat.

11 WINEGLASS
A tall, slightly
rounded,
stemmed glass
for wine-based
cocktails. White
wine glasses are a
fine substitute for
highball glasses
and are also good
for frozen drinks.
Balloon-shaped
red wine glasses
are ideal for fruity
cocktails as
well as punches.

HOME BAR TOOLS

1   2   3   4   5   6

1 HAWTHORNE STRAINER

The best all-purpose strainer. A semicircular spring ensures a spill-proof fit on a shaker. Look for a tightly coiled spring, which keeps muddled fruit and herbs out of drinks.

2 JIGGER

A two-sided stainless steel measuring instrument for precise mixing.

Look for one with ½- and 1-ounce cups. A shot glass with measures works well, too.

3 MUDDLER

A sturdy tool that's used to crush herbs, sugar cubes and fresh fruit; it's traditionally made of wood. Choose a muddler that can reach the bottom of a cocktail shaker; in a pinch, substitute a long-handled wooden spoon.

4 CHANNEL KNIFE

A small, spoon-shaped knife with a metal tooth. Creates garnishes by turning citrus-fruit peels into long, thin twists.

5 JULEP STRAINER

The preferred device for straining cocktails from a pint glass because it fits securely. Fine holes keep ice out of the drink.

6 HAND JUICER

A metal or ceramic citrus press, available in a variety of sizes, that allows you to squeeze lemons, limes and oranges *à la minute.*

7 WAITER'S CORKSCREW

A pocketknife-like tool with a bottle opener and a blade for cutting foil from wine caps. Bartenders prefer it to bulkier, more complicated corkscrews.

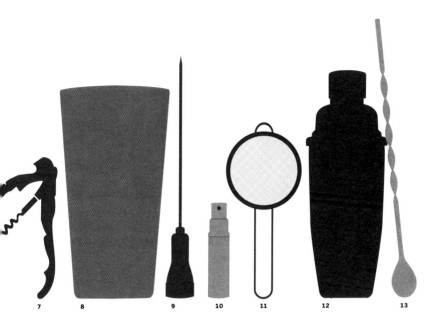

7   8   9   10   11   12   13

8 BOSTON SHAKER

The bartender's choice, consisting of a pint glass with a metal canister that covers the glass to create a seal. Add ingredients to the glass; shake with the metal half pointing away from you.

9 ICE PICK

A sharp metal tool with a sturdy handle used to break off chunks from a larger block of ice.

10 ATOMIZER

A small spray bottle used to disperse tiny quantities of aromatic liquid evenly over the surface of an empty glass or on top of a cocktail. (Popular in the 1950s, when glasses spritzed with vermouth for extra-dry martinis were all the rage.) Little spray bottles are widely available at drugstores.

11 FINE STRAINER

A fine-mesh strainer, normally used for tea preparation; it's placed over a glass before the cocktail is poured in (see Straining Drinks on p. 16). Ideal for keeping unwanted bits of muddled herbs, fruit and crushed ice out of drinks, resulting in a perfectly clear cocktail.

12 COBBLER SHAKER

The most commonly used shaker, with a metal cup for mixing drinks with ice, a built-in strainer and a fitted top.

13 BAR SPOON

A long-handled metal spoon that mixes cocktails without creating air bubbles. Also useful to measure small amounts of liquid (1 bar spoon equals about 1 teaspoon).

BEGINNER'S COCKTAIL GUIDE

Essential mixers and super-simple drinks

THE NEW BAR PANTRY

DRY & SWEET VERMOUTHS
For martinis and Manhattans, store 375-ml bottles of these vermouths in your fridge. The small bottles take up less space than the usual 750-ml ones.

TRIPLE SEC
Good triple sec is essential for margaritas, cosmos and sidecars. Beware of artificially flavored versions. Cointreau, Combier and Marie Brizard are all good brands.

CAMPARI OR APEROL
Mixed with club soda or Prosecco, these brightly colored bittersweet aperitifs make great simple cocktails before a meal.

ANGOSTURA & PEYCHAUD'S BITTERS
Aromatic bitters are the salt and pepper of cocktails. Angostura adds spicy notes like cinnamon and allspice; Peychaud's contributes bright cranberry and fennel tones to drinks like the classic Sazerac.

AMARO
Bittersweet *amari* (Italian for "bitter") are sipped after dinner to help digestion. They also work well in small quantities in cocktails like the rye-based Blackened Orange (p. 102). Amaro Nonino is a good all-around choice.

ORGEAT
This sweet, orange flower–accented almond syrup is a secret weapon for rum drinks, adding bright marzipan notes.

BÉNÉDICTINE
Created more than 500 years ago, this versatile herbal liqueur adds complexity to drinks made with brown spirits like Cognac, Scotch, rye and añejo tequila.

GREEN CHARTREUSE
A favorite among bartenders, this potent spirit is made from more than 100 different Alpine herbs and plants. It's a great addition to spicy botanical spirits like gin, aquavit and tequila.

ST-GERMAIN ELDERFLOWER LIQUEUR
Another bartender's favorite, this low-proof liqueur is super-versatile, adding brightness to brown and bitter drinks and sweet, floral, fruity accents to clear-spirited cocktails.

SIMPLE RECIPES FOR COCKTAIL NOVICES

AIR MAIL
Citrusy rum-spiked
Champagne cocktail
P. 80

APPLES TO ORANGES
Bourbon drink with a
surprise ingredient **P. 98**

COLD SPRING COCKTAIL
Maple-sweetened
Cognac sour **P. 113**

CORK COUNTY BUBBLES
Irish whiskey–spiked
Champagne drink **P. 92**

DEMPSEY
Apple-y gin cocktail **P. 58**

DOMINICANA
Rum, coffee liqueur and
whipped cream **P. 88**

THE DON'S BRAMBLE
Blackberry-and-pisco
refresher **P. 110**

GAELIC PUNCH
Hot whiskey drink **P. 124**

**GEORGIAN BRANDY
PUNCH**
Iced Cognac punch
P. 124

LUSH CAR
Vodka sidecar with
Cognac and berries **P. 42**

MARGARITA
Lime-and-tequila
classic **P. 64**

MARTINEZ
Slightly sweet cousin to
the dry gin martini **P. 58**

OAXACA OLD-FASHIONED
Tequila-and-mezcal take
on a classic **P. 70**

PALOMA
Fizzy tequila-and-
grapefruit drink **P. 62**

PAMPLEMOUSSE
Gin-and-grapefruit
brunch cocktail **P. 48**

STRAWBERRY SHAG
Strawberry-lemon-
vodka cooler **P. 36**

VIXEN
Sweet-tart vodka
aperitif **P. 42**

PARTY ADVICE FROM A STAR MIXOLOGIST

"COCKTAIL PARTY GUESTS OFTEN BRING THEIR FAVORITE SPIRITS—
RUM, VODKA, WHISKEY. BY STOCKING UP ON MIXERS LIKE
VERMOUTHS, LIQUEURS, BITTERS, NATURAL SODAS AND FRESH
CITRUS JUICES, YOU'LL ALWAYS BE READY TO MAKE DRINKS
EVERYONE WILL LOVE." — Jim Meehan, PDT, Manhattan

MIXOLOGY BASICS

MAKING A TWIST

A twist—a small piece of citrus zest—adds concentrated citrus flavor from the peel's essential oils.

TO MAKE AND USE A STANDARD TWIST
1 Use a sharp paring knife or vegetable peeler to cut a thin, oval, quarter-size disk of the peel, avoiding the pith.
2 Grasp the outer edges skin side down between the thumb and two fingers and pinch the twist over the drink. Rub the peel around the rim of the glass and drop it into the drink.

TO MAKE A SPIRAL-CUT TWIST
1 Use a channel knife to cut a 3-inch-long piece of peel with some of the pith intact (this helps the spiral hold its shape). It's best to cut the twist over the glass so the essential oils from the peel fall into the drink.
2 Wrap the twist around a straw or a chopstick and tighten at both ends to create a curlicue shape.

SMACKING HERBS

To accentuate the aroma of fresh herbs used for garnish, hold the herbs in one hand. Clap with the other hand to release the essential oils stored in the plant leaves.

FLAMING A TWIST

Flaming a lemon or orange twist caramelizes the zest's essential oils.

1 Cut a thin, oval, quarter-size piece of peel with a bit of the pith intact.
2 Gently grasp the outer edges skin side down between the thumb and two fingers and hold the twist about 4 inches over the cocktail.
3 Hold a lit match over the drink an inch away from the twist—don't let the flame touch the peel—then pinch the edges of the twist sharply so that the citrus oil falls through the flame and into the drink.

STRAINING DRINKS

Drinks made with muddled fruit and herbs are sometimes double strained to remove tiny particles, so the cocktail is pristine and clear.

1 Place a fine tea strainer over the serving glass.
2 Make the drink in a shaker or pint glass, then set a Hawthorne or julep strainer on top and pour the drink through both strainers into the serving glass.

RIMMING A GLASS

Bartenders often coat only half of the rim of a glass so there's a choice of sides to sip from.

1 Spread a few tablespoonfuls of salt (preferably kosher), sugar or other powdered or very finely crushed ingredient on a small plate.
2 Moisten the outer rim of the glass with a citrus-fruit wedge, water or a syrup or colorful liquid like pomegranate juice. Then roll the outer rim of the glass on the plate until lightly coated.
3 Hold the glass upside down and tap to release any excess.

PERFECTING ICE

Ice is essential to preparing a drink. For serving most drinks, the bigger the pieces, the better. Large chunks of ice melt more slowly, and dilute drinks less. Detail-obsessed bars like Rob Roy in Seattle and Weather Up Tribeca in New York City cut crystal-clear ice from large blocks into cubes, long spears and spheres. The exception to the big-ice rule: the crushed ice in juleps and swizzled drinks. Besides melting quickly, which dilutes potent drinks, crushed ice also adds an appealing

frost to glasses. Cracked ice is used for stirring. It helps to cool down a drink more quickly than stirring with standard-size ice cubes.

TO MAKE BIG BLOCKS OF ICE FOR PUNCH BOWLS, pour water into a large, shallow plastic container and freeze. To unmold, first warm the bottom of the container in hot water.

TO MAKE EXTRA-LARGE ICE CUBES FOR ROCKS GLASSES, use flexible silicone ice molds (available at cocktailkingdom.com). Or make a large block of ice in a loaf pan and use an ice pick to break off chunks the size you want.

TO MAKE CRUSHED ICE, cover cubes in a clean kitchen towel and pound with a wooden hammer or rolling pin.

TO MAKE CRACKED ICE, place an ice cube in the palm of your hand and tap it with the back of a bar spoon until it breaks into pieces.

TO MAKE COMPLETELY CLEAR CUBES, fill ice trays with hot filtered water.

TO MAKE PERFECTLY SQUARE CUBES, use flexible silicone Perfect Cube ice trays (available at surlatable.com).

HOMEMADE MIXERS

SIMPLE SYRUP

This bar staple is essential to many well-balanced cocktails. It's good to keep a jar of the syrup stashed in your refrigerator.

MAKES ABOUT 12 OUNCES
In a small saucepan, bring 8 ounces water and 1 cup sugar to a boil over moderately high heat, stirring until the sugar dissolves. Let cool, cover and refrigerate for up to 1 month.

RICH SIMPLE SYRUP

Demerara sugar gives this concentrated syrup a great molasses flavor.

MAKES ABOUT 8 OUNCES
In a small saucepan, bring 4 ounces water and 1 cup Demerara sugar to a boil over moderately high heat, stirring until the sugar dissolves. Let cool, cover and refrigerate for up to 1 month.

EASIEST SIMPLE SYRUP

This extremely easy simple syrup, made without a stove, is an old bartender's trick.

MAKES ABOUT 12 OUNCES
In a bottle or jar with a tight-fitting lid, shake 8 ounces hot water with 1 cup superfine sugar. Let cool and refrigerate for up to 1 month.

HOMEMADE GRENADINE

This tangy, pomegranate-flavored mixer adds color and sweetness to drinks. For a tarter syrup, decrease the sugar by half.

MAKES ABOUT 12 OUNCES
In a bottle or jar with a tight-fitting lid, shake 8 ounces unsweetened pomegranate juice with 1 cup sugar until the sugar dissolves. If desired, add 1/8 teaspoon orange flower water. Refrigerate for up to 2 weeks.

A WORD ON HONEY & AGAVE *Natural sweeteners like honey and agave nectar impart a more complex flavor than simple syrup. To make a pourable syrup, warm honey or agave nectar, then mix it with an equal part of water. Or simply stir equal parts of the sweetener and hot water in a jar. For a richer syrup, use twice as much sweetener as water. Let the syrup cool before using it in drinks.*

CONVERSION CHARTS

CUPS	OUNCES	LITERS
4¼ CUPS	34 OUNCES	1 LITER
4 CUPS	32 OUNCES	
3 CUPS	24 OUNCES	
2 CUPS	16 OUNCES	
1 CUP	8 OUNCES	
¾ CUP	6 OUNCES	
½ CUP	4 OUNCES	
¼ CUP	2 OUNCES	60 MILLILITERS

TABLESPOONS	OUNCES	MILLILITERS
2 TABLESPOONS	1 OUNCE	30 MILLILITERS
1½ TABLESPOONS	¾ OUNCE	
4 TEASPOONS	⅔ OUNCE	20 MILLILITERS
1 TABLESPOON	½ OUNCE	15 MILLILITERS
2 TEASPOONS	⅓ OUNCE	10 MILLILITERS
1½ TEASPOONS	¼ OUNCE	

ESSENTIAL SPIRITS

Mixologists
are using more
and more
esoteric spirits
in their drinks,
but these five
choices are
still the backbone
of a great
cocktail list.

GIN

A dry, clear spirit, gin is
distilled with such
botanicals as juniper,
coriander, cardamom
and dried citrus peel,
which often add piney,
spicy or citrusy notes.
Ubiquitous dry gin, also
known as **LONDON DRY**,
is bolder in flavor than
the slightly sweet, less
botanically intense
OLD TOM style. Distilled
with sweet orange
peel, **PLYMOUTH GIN**
tastes sweeter than
spicy London Dry. The
"official" gin of the
British Royal Navy for
nearly two centuries,
Plymouth may be
produced only in
Plymouth, England.

VODKA

Produced all over the
world, vodka is
traditionally distilled
from fermented grain
or potatoes, but nearly
any fruit or vegetable
that contains starch or
sugar can be used,
from grapes to beets.
The finest flavored
vodkas are often made
with fruit-infused
grain alcohol that's run
through a pot still.

20

FOOD & WINE

TEQUILA

The best examples of this agave-based spirit are made with 100 percent blue agave. **BLANCO** tequila is aged for up to two months. **REPOSADO** ("rested") tequila will sit for up to one year. **AÑEJO** ("aged") tequila ages for up to three years. **MEZCAL,** also agave-based, has a smoky flavor that comes from roasting the agave hearts in earthen pits before fermentation. The finest mezcal is made in Mexico's Oaxaca region.

WHISKEY

This spirit is distilled from a fermented mash of grains and aged in wood barrels. (Whiskey is spelled without an "e" in Scotland, Canada and Japan.) **BOURBON,** which tastes of brown sugar and toffee, is distilled primarily from corn. **RYE** whiskey, which is made with a minimum of 51 percent rye, is more grassy. **SCOTCH** is made in two major styles: **single malts,** produced from 100 percent malted barley from one distillery; and **blends,** a mixture of single-malt and grain whisky from more than one distillery.

RUM

Distilled from cane syrup, molasses or fresh pressed sugarcane, rums are primarily produced in tropical regions. **WHITE** rums typically age for a short time in wood. **DARK** rums, especially Jamaican ones, tend to be rich and flavorful. **AÑEJO** rums are barrel-aged and extra smooth. **RHUM AGRICOLE** is made in the French West Indies from fresh pressed sugarcane juice (not syrup or molasses).

SPIRITS LEXICON

ABSINTHE An anise-flavored spirit formerly banned in the United States. It's flavored with such botanicals as wormwood, green anise and fennel seeds.

AGAVE NECTAR A rich, sweet syrup made from the sap of the cactus-like agave plant.

AMARO A bittersweet Italian herbal liqueur often served as an after-dinner drink.

APEROL A low-proof Italian aperitif flavored with bitter orange, rhubarb and gentian.

APPLE BRANDY A distilled fermented apple cider that is aged in oak barrels. Most of the brandy is bottled at 80 proof, but **BONDED** apple brandy, which is preferable in cocktails because of its concentrated green-apple flavor, is 100 proof.

APPLEJACK An American apple brandy that's blended with neutral spirits.

AQUAVIT A clear, grain- or potato-based Scandinavian spirit flavored with caraway seeds and other botanicals, such as fennel, anise and citrus peel.

BÉNÉDICTINE A brandy-based herbal liqueur derived from a recipe developed by a French monk in 1510.

BITTERS A concentrated tincture of bitter and aromatic herbs, roots and spices that adds complexity to drinks.

Varieties include orange, grapefruit, rhubarb and aromatic bitters, the best known of which is **ANGOSTURA,** created in Angostura, Venezuela, in 1824. Germany's **BITTER TRUTH** (photo below) makes bitters in traditional flavors as well as unusual ones like celery and chocolate. **FEE BROTHERS** bitters, which come in 12 flavors, have been made in Rochester, New York, for more than 60 years. **PEYCHAUD'S** bitters have bright anise and cranberry flavors; the recipe dates to 19th-century New Orleans.

BONAL GENTIANE-QUINA A slightly bitter French aperitif wine infused with gentian root and cinchona bark, which contains quinine.

BONDED WHISKEY A whiskey that's been produced by a single distillery, distilled during a single season, aged a minimum of four years, bottled at 100 proof and stored in a "bonded" warehouse under U.S. government supervision.

CACHAÇA A potent Brazilian spirit distilled from sugarcane juice.

CALVADOS A cask-aged brandy made in the Normandy region of France from apples and sometimes pears.

CAMPARI A potent, bright red Italian aperitif made from fruit, herbs and spices.

CANE SYRUP A very sweet, thick syrup made by evaporating the water from sugarcane juice.

CARPANO ANTICA FORMULA A rich and complex crimson-colored sweet Italian vermouth.

CHARTREUSE A spicy French herbal liqueur made from more than 100 botanicals; **GREEN** Chartreuse is more potent than the honey-sweetened **YELLOW** one.

COCCHI APERITIVO AMERICANO A low-alcohol, wine-based aperitif infused with citrus, herbs such as gentian and quinine-rich cinchona bark.

COGNAC An oak-aged brandy made from grapes grown in France's Charente region. **VSOP** (Very Superior Old Pale) Cognac must be aged a minimum of four years in French oak barrels.

COINTREAU A French triple sec that is made by macerating and distilling sun-dried sweet and bitter orange peels.

CRÉOLE SHRUBB A rum-based orange liqueur flavored with Creole spices and bitter orange peels.

CURAÇAO A general term for orange-flavored liqueurs produced in the French West Indies.

CYNAR A pleasantly bitter Italian liqueur made from 13 herbs and plants, including artichokes.

DIMMI A fruity and floral liqueur infused with licorice, vanilla, bitter orange and peach.

DRAMBUIE A whisky-based Scottish liqueur flavored with honey, herbs and spices.

DUBONNET A wine-based, quinine-enhanced aperitif that comes in two varieties. The **ROUGE** is full-bodied. The drier **BLANC** is a good substitute for dry vermouth.

EAU-DE-VIE A clear, unaged fruit brandy. Classic varieties include **FRAMBOISE** (raspberry), **POIRE** (pear), **ABRICOT** (apricot), **KIRSCH** (cherry) and **MIRABELLE** (plum).

FERNET-BRANCA A potent, bitter Italian digestif made from 27 herbs.

GENEVER A clear, botanically rich, malted grain–based spirit from Holland. **OUDE** refers to the maltier old-style; lighter, less malty versions are called **JONGE.**

GRENADINE A sweet red syrup made from pomegranate juice and sugar (see the Homemade Grenadine recipe on p. 18).

GUM SYRUP A simple syrup that's been thickened with gum arabic, a natural gum made from the sap of acacia trees.

HEERING CHERRY LIQUEUR A Danish brandy-based cherry liqueur.

LICOR 43 A citrus-and-vanilla-flavored Spanish liqueur made from a combination of 43 herbs and spices.

LILLET A wine-based French aperitif flavored with orange peel and quinine. The lesser-known **ROUGE** variety is sweeter than the more widely available **BLANC.**

MADEIRA A fortified wine from the island of Madeira, usually named for one of four grape varieties: **SERCIAL** (the driest), **VERDELHO, BUAL** or **MALMSEY,** which are progressively sweeter.

MARASCHINO LIQUEUR A clear Italian liqueur, the best of which is distilled from sour marasca cherries and their pits, aged in ash barrels, then sweetened with sugar.

ORGEAT A sweet, nonalcoholic syrup made from almonds or almond extract, sugar and rose or orange flower water.

PERNOD A French producer of a liqueur made from the essential oils of star anise and fennel combined with herbs, spices, sugar and a neutral spirit. Pernod recently rereleased their absinthe, which, like all absinthes, had been banned in the United States since 1912.

PIMM'S NO. 1 A gin-based English aperitif often served with ginger beer or lemonade.

24

PISCO A clear brandy distilled from grapes in the wine-producing regions of Peru and Chile.

PORT A fortified wine from the Douro region of Portugal. Styles include fruity, young **RUBY** port; richer, nuttier **TAWNY;** thick-textured, oak-aged **LATE BOTTLED VINTAGE (LBV);** and decadent **VINTAGE** port, made from the best grapes in the best vintages. Dry **WHITE** port is often served chilled, as an aperitif.

PUNT E MES A spicy, orange-accented sweet Italian vermouth fortified with bitters.

SHERRY A fortified wine from Spain's Jerez region. Varieties include dry styles like **FINO** and **MANZANILLA;** nuttier, richer **AMONTILLADO** and **OLOROSO;** and viscous sweet **PEDRO XIMÉNEZ (PX)** and **CREAM** sherry. **EAST INDIA** sherry falls between an oloroso and a PX in style.

SLOE GIN A bittersweet liqueur produced by infusing gin or a neutral spirit with sloe berries and sugar.

ST. ELIZABETH ALLSPICE DRAM An Austrian rum-based liqueur infused with Jamaican allspice berries.

ST-GERMAIN ELDERFLOWER LIQUEUR A French liqueur made by blending macerated elderflower blossoms with eau-de-vie. It has hints of pear, peach and grapefruit zest.

STREGA An Italian liqueur infused with about 70 herbs and spices, including saffron, which gives it a golden yellow color.

TRIPLE SEC An orange-flavored liqueur that is similar to curaçao but not as sweet. Cointreau, created in France in 1875, is the most famous.

VELVET FALERNUM A low-alcohol, sugarcane-based liqueur from Barbados flavored with clove, almond and lime.

VERMOUTH An aromatic fortified wine. The **DRY** variety (photo at left) is used in martinis. **SWEET** vermouth, which is usually red, is often used for Manhattans. **BIANCO,** or **BLANC,** vermouth is an aromatic, sweet white vermouth traditionally served on the rocks.

ZWACK An intense Hungarian herbal liqueur produced since 1790 from a secret blend of more than 40 herbs and spices.

COCKTAIL TRENDS: WHAT'S HOT, WHAT'S NOT

IN

OUT

1 TEA DRINKS
It was only a matter of time before the tea trend had an impact on cocktails. Try steeping vodka with black tea for a bit of astringency, as in the Tea Thyme (p. 34), or green tea for nutty flavors.

2 SODA FOUNTAIN–INSPIRED DRINKS
Restaurants and bars across the country are serving carbonated drinks flavored with mixers like syrups and marmalade (see the Bitter Orange & Black Pepper Soda, p. 170).

3 SALTED COCKTAILS
Salt has moved beyond margaritas. A pinch adds complexity to drinks, especially ones with citrus notes, like the Silver Monk (p. 68).

4 CHEFS' COCKTAILS
Top chefs are infatuated with cocktails. They're teaming up with mixologists to create drinks using unorthodox ingredients, such as the fresh chiles in the Porch Crawler (p. 150).

5 VINEGAR IN THE MIX
Once popular in Colonial America, vinegar-spiked drinks are making a comeback. Autumn in New York (p. 142) gets a sweet-tart tang from apple cider vinegar.

1 HIPSTER BARTENDERS
When cocktail culture became cool, it attracted bartenders just looking to cash in. Now, committed professionals dominate the scene.

2 HIGH-TECH COCKTAILS
Unless you're Chicago star chef Grant Achatz, you're probably not successfully using molecular gastronomy techniques to turn drinks into hors d'oeuvres.

3 HOUSE-MADE BITTERS
Most serious bartenders are now focused on making drinks instead of ingredients; they're buying great bitters rather than creating their own.

4 FREE-POURED COCKTAILS
Preparing a cocktail is like baking a cake: Exact measurements yield well-balanced results. The best bartenders use a jigger.

5 MEATY DRINKS
As America's pork obsession has finally subsided, we think it's safe to say good-bye to bacon-rimmed glasses.

A SEASONAL DRINK FOR EVERY MONTH

JANUARY	FEBRUARY	MARCH
PEAR BALM Ripe pear and green tea in a no-alcohol aperitif **P. 166**	**SASSENACH PUNCH** Smoky Scotch-based punch with blood orange juice **P. 122**	**DOMINICANA** Whipped cream–topped White Russian variation **P. 88**

APRIL	MAY	JUNE
BRIDAL SHOWER Vodka-spiked rhubarb soda **P. 140**	**LAST-STRAW COBBLER** Strawberry slushie for grown-ups **P. 72**	**STRAWBERRY SHAG** Basil-scented vodka-lemon cooler **P. 36**

JULY	AUGUST	SEPTEMBER
CALIFORNIA COLLINS Lemon verbena collins **P. 52**	**AUGUST COLLINS** Raspberry-Scotch combo **P. 94**	**THE DON'S BRAMBLE** Late-summer blackberry refresher **P. 110**

OCTOBER	NOVEMBER	DECEMBER
THE HEIRLOOM Licorice-scented gin cocktail with fresh Concord grapes **P. 153**	**CAFÉ BRÛLOT FLIP** Rich, spicy after-dinner drink **P. 116**	**CHAMPAGNE HOLIDAY PUNCH** Pineapple-genever sparkler for a crowd **P. 123**

VODKA

LEFT TO RIGHT: Celery Cup No. 1, P. 38; Bloody Good Balsamic Mary, P. 39

Gold "Orsini" tea light holder from the Conran Shop; "Roost" highball glass from Global Table; tumbler from ABC Carpet & Home.

KATHY CASEY

"Vodka is the perfect foundation for creative drinks," says chef, mixologist and restaurant consultant Kathy Casey. In the early '90s, Casey became a pioneer in crafting thoughtful cocktails using the best seasonal ingredients in her restaurant kitchens. Today she mixes vodka and other spirits with everything from fresh pineapple, cilantro and jalapeño (p. 40) to honey from her hive. You can watch her in action on her new show, *Kathy Casey's Liquid Kitchen,* on smallscreennetwork.com.

❤ Platinum Sparkle

Ice
1½ ounces vodka
 ½ ounce maraschino
     liqueur
 ½ ounce Lillet blanc
 ½ ounce fresh lemon juice
 ½ ounce brut Champagne
  1 brandied or maraschino
     cherry, for garnish

For parties, Casey premixes the first four ingredients in large batches (3 parts vodka to 1 part each liqueur, Lillet and lemon juice). When she's ready to pour, she fills a shaker with ice and 3 ounces of the mixture, shakes, strains into a glass and tops with Champagne.

Fill a cocktail shaker with ice. Add the vodka, liqueur, Lillet and lemon juice; shake well. Strain into a chilled martini glass or flute and stir in the Champagne. Garnish with the cherry.

Platinum Sparkle

"Paloma" Champagne
flutes from
Crate & Barrel.

"KALEIDO" WALLPAPER FROM WALLPAPER COLLECTIVE.

VODKA

 ## Mango Moscow Mule

Ice
1½ ounces vodka
2 ounces mango nectar or juice
½ ounce fresh lime juice
2 ounces chilled ginger beer
1 slice of candied ginger skewered on a pick and 1 lime wheel, for garnish

To give this drink extra mango flavor, Casey sometimes adds muddled chunks of fresh mango with the fruit nectar.

Fill a cocktail shaker with ice. Add the vodka, mango nectar and lime juice and shake well. Strain into an ice-filled collins glass and stir in the ginger beer. Garnish with the candied ginger and lime wheel.

 ## Ginger Persuasion

4 blueberries
Ice
1 ounce vodka
½ ounce ginger liqueur
½ ounce aquavit
1 tablespoon honey, preferably lavender honey
2 dashes of Angostura bitters
1 ounce sparkling Pinot Noir or other red sparkling wine

Casey's friend Anu Apte, owner of Rob Roy in Seattle, created this unconventional drink with dry, slightly tannic sparkling Pinot Noir and sweet blueberries, honey and ginger liqueur. The red wine looks gorgeous floating on the bluish-beige cocktail.

In a cocktail shaker, muddle the berries. Add ice and the vodka, ginger liqueur, aquavit, honey and bitters and shake well. Pour through a fine strainer into a chilled flute and float the sparkling wine on top.

VODKA

♇ Tuscan Martini

¼ ounce dry white vermouth
¼ ounce grappa
1 lemon twist
Ice
3 ounces vodka
1 rosemary sprig and 1 olive skewered on a pick, for garnish

Although mixologists typically stir martinis to keep them clear, Casey shakes hers, which adds bubbles and results in attractive ice shards on the surface of the drink. She likes to garnish this lemony martini with an olive that's been marinating with sliced lemons, garlic, olive oil and rosemary.

In a cocktail shaker, combine the vermouth and grappa. Pinch the twist over the shaker and drop it in. Shake well, then discard the mixture. Fill the rinsed shaker with ice. Add the vodka and shake well. Strain into a martini glass and garnish with the rosemary sprig and skewered olive.

VODKA

Tea Thyme

TEA VODKA

TIME: 2 HR INFUSING

- 12 ounces vodka
- 1 English Breakfast tea bag

COCKTAIL

- 2 thyme sprigs
- Ice
- 1½ ounces Tea Vodka
- ¾ ounce fresh lemon juice
- 2 teaspoons honey mixed with 2 teaspoons warm water

"Local honey is a great way to customize your cocktails," says Casey. She often uses the dark, fig-flavored honey from her studio's backyard hive (which sits under a fig tree). She also sells it at kathycasey.com/shop.

1 MAKE THE TEA VODKA In a jar, combine the vodka with the tea bag. Let stand at room temperature for 2 hours, then discard the tea bag. (Leftover infused vodka can be kept at room temperature for up to 1 month.)

2 MAKE THE COCKTAIL In a cocktail shaker, lightly muddle 1 of the thyme sprigs. Add ice and the 1½ ounces of Tea Vodka, the lemon juice and the honey syrup and shake well. Strain into a chilled martini glass or coupe and garnish with the remaining thyme sprig.

Tea Thyme

*"Fern" Champagne saucer
by William Yeoward.*

VODKA

 ## Rosemary's Club

1 small rosemary sprig
1 ounce vodka
1 ounce gin
¾ ounce fresh lemon juice
½ ounce Simple Syrup
   (p. 18)
1 large egg white
5 raspberries, plus 3
   raspberries skewered
   on a pick for garnish
Ice

In her vodka-fortified twist on a vintage gin drink called the Clover Club, Casey replaces the raspberry syrup with fresh raspberries and simple syrup and adds fragrant muddled rosemary.

In a cocktail shaker, lightly muddle the rosemary. Add the vodka, gin, lemon juice, Simple Syrup, egg white and the 5 raspberries; shake well. Add ice and shake again. Strain into a chilled martini glass and garnish with the skewered berries.

 ## Strawberry Shag

3 strawberries, halved,
   plus 1 strawberry for
   garnish
2 large basil sprigs, plus
   1 small basil leaf for
   garnish
Ice
1½ ounces vodka
1 ounce fresh lemon juice
¾ ounce Simple Syrup
   (p. 18)
3 ounces chilled club
   soda

This recipe is from Casey's 2009 book *Sips & Apps*. She improves the classic combination of strawberries, lemonade and vodka—already a terrific summer cooler—by adding fresh basil.

In a cocktail shaker, muddle the halved strawberries with the basil sprigs. Add ice and the vodka, lemon juice and Simple Syrup; shake well. Strain into an ice-filled collins glass. Stir in the club soda and garnish with the strawberry and basil leaf.

Rosemary's Club

"Tifone" tray by Armani/Casa; "Bossa Nova" martini glass by Nachtmann for Riedel.

VODKA

 ## Celery Cup No. 1

One 2-inch piece of celery,
plus 1 small leafy celery
rib for garnish

3 thin slices of English
cucumber

¼ cup chopped cilantro

1 ounce fresh lemon juice

Ice

1½ ounces cucumber
vodka or plain vodka

½ ounce Pimm's No. 1
(English gin-based
aperitif)

¾ ounce agave nectar

H. Joseph Ehrmann, owner of the excellent
San Francisco bar Elixir, devised this
variation on the Pimm's Cup. Use celery ribs
that are close to the heart; they're less
stringy and milder in flavor than outer ribs.

In a cocktail shaker, muddle the piece
of celery with the cucumber slices,
cilantro and lemon juice. Add ice and
the vodka, Pimm's and agave nectar
and shake well. Strain the drink into an
ice-filled collins or highball glass and
garnish with the celery rib.

VODKA

 ## Bloody Good Balsamic Mary

Ice
1½ ounces Bloody Good
Vodka (below) or plain
vodka
4 ounces Balsamic Mary
Mix (below)
1 ounce fresh lemon juice
3 cherry tomatoes
skewered on a pick,
1 lemon wedge,
1 rosemary sprig, olives
and/or slivers
of salami, for garnish

Although Casey's balsamic-spiked Bloody
Mary mix is supertasty, you can simplify this
recipe by using a store-bought mix.

Fill a large collins glass with ice. Add the
vodka, Balsamic Mary Mix and lemon
juice and stir well. Garnish as desired.

BLOODY GOOD VODKA
TIME: 24 HR INFUSING

In a large jar, combine 12 ounces vodka,
¼ cup chopped sun-dried tomatoes (not
oil-packed), ½ teaspoon whole black
peppercorns and 1 garlic clove. Cover; let
stand for 24 hours. Strain into a clean
jar, pressing on the solids. Refrigerate for
up to 6 months. Makes about 12 ounces.

BALSAMIC MARY MIX

In a large jar, mix 12 ounces tomato juice,
¾ ounce balsamic vinegar, ½ ounce
fresh lemon juice, ½ ounce Worcestershire
sauce, 1½ teaspoons horseradish,
¼ teaspoon kosher salt and a large pinch
of freshly ground pepper. Refrigerate
for up to 1 week. Makes about 14 ounces.

VODKA

 ## Pineapple Pico

1 lime wedge and kosher salt

Ice

1 ounce pineapple vodka or plain vodka

1 ounce blanco tequila

½ ounce Cointreau or other triple sec

1 ounce fresh lime juice

¾ ounce agave nectar

1 pineapple leaf, for garnish (optional)

2 tablespoons Pineapple Pico de Gallo (below), for garnish

Pineapple pico de gallo, a spicy fresh relish, adds flavor and texture to this tropical drink. (Casey serves the cocktail with an extra-fat straw.) Serve any leftover pico de gallo with grilled fish or shrimp, on top of ice cream or panna cotta or as a dip with chips.

Moisten the outer rim of a collins or highball glass with the lime wedge and coat lightly with salt. Add ice to the glass. Fill a cocktail shaker with ice, then add all of the remaining ingredients except the garnishes; shake well. Strain into the prepared glass and garnish with the pineapple leaf and Pineapple Pico de Gallo.

PINEAPPLE PICO DE GALLO

In a small bowl, combine ¼ cup pineapple jam with ¾ cup diced pineapple, ¼ cup diced strawberries, 2 tablespoons chopped cilantro and 1 tablespoon minced jalapeño. Refrigerate, covered, for up to 2 days. Makes about 1¼ cups.

Pineapple Pico

"Silodesign" double-wall highball glass from Unica Home;
"Rolo" shot glass from Crate & Barrel.

VODKA

♼ Lush Car

Ice
1½ ounces vodka
 ½ ounce Cognac
 ½ ounce fresh lemon juice
 ½ ounce Simple Syrup
     (p. 18)
 5 blackberries
 1 orange twist, for
     garnish

Casey lightens the sidecar by replacing most of the traditional Cognac with vodka and adding muddled fresh blackberries. For an extra hint of citrusy complexity, she sometimes includes a drop of orange blossom water, too.

Fill a cocktail shaker with ice. Add the vodka, Cognac, lemon juice, Simple Syrup and blackberries and shake well. Strain into a chilled martini glass and garnish with the orange twist.

♼ Vixen

Ice
1½ ounces vodka
 ¾ ounce Aperol (bitter
     orange Italian aperitif)
 ½ ounce St-Germain
     elderflower liqueur
 1 lemon twist, for garnish

In the summer, Casey likes to serve this aperitif alongside pitted fresh Bing cherries topped with goat cheese and slivered toasted almonds. When she makes the Vixen, she uses a channel knife (p. 12) to cut the lemon twist over the drink so the citrus oil spritzes onto the surface.

Fill a pint glass with ice. Add the vodka, Aperol and St-Germain and stir well. Strain into a chilled martini glass and garnish with the lemon twist.

VODKA

■ Hibiscus Punch

MAKES ABOUT 12 DRINKS

- 1 cup dried hibiscus flowers or loose hibiscus tea
- 48 ounces boiling water
- 1½ cups honey
- 32 ounces vodka
- 8 ounces fresh lime juice
- 4 ounces pineapple juice
- 1 teaspoon Angostura bitters

Ice

Lime wheels, for garnish

"I love punches for large parties because you can make them ahead of time," says Casey. Dried hibiscus flowers, also called *flor de Jamaica,* give this punch a tart, exotic flavor and a fabulous magenta color. They also make a beautiful garnish. The flowers can be found at Latin and Caribbean markets and at health food stores.

In a large heatproof bowl, cover the hibiscus flowers with the boiling water and let steep for 10 minutes. Strain into a large heatproof jar, stir in the honey and let cool; refrigerate the flowers. Stir the vodka into the hibiscus liquid and refrigerate until chilled, about 2 hours or up to 4 days. Stir in the lime juice, pineapple juice and bitters. Pour into ice-filled double rocks glasses and garnish with the hibiscus flowers and lime wheels.

LEFT TO RIGHT: California Collins, P. 52; Pamplemousse, P. 48

"Harmonie" ice bucket by Baccarat; "Carat" highball glasses by Orrefors; "Abysse" American red wine glass no. 2 by Baccarat.

GIN

RYAN FITZGERALD

"Gin is incredible for bartenders to work with," says Ryan Fitzgerald, spirits and cocktail consultant at San Francisco's Beretta and former bartender at the speakeasy-style Bourbon & Branch. "Sometimes it stands out in a drink; other times it integrates all the other ingredients." He's especially excited about many of the new and varied gins on the market, with subtle flavors ranging from cucumber and rose petals to coriander and ginger.

🍸 English Harvest

Ice
- 1 ounce London dry gin
- ¾ ounce bonded apple brandy
- ¾ ounce dry vermouth
- ¾ ounce unfiltered apple juice
- ¼ ounce orgeat (almond-flavored syrup)
- 3 dashes of Angostura bitters
- 1 spiral-cut orange twist (p. 16), for garnish

Fitzgerald felt inspired to create this spicy fall cocktail after eating apples with peanut butter—a combination he loves but that wouldn't quite work in a drink. His solution was to mix almond syrup (available at most coffee shops) with apple juice and fiery apple brandy.

Fill a cocktail shaker with ice. Add all of the remaining ingredients except the garnish and shake well. Strain into a small chilled coupe or snifter and garnish with the orange twist.

English Harvest

"Mitos" Cognac glass
by Květná from TableArt.

"GOLDONI" WALLPAPER BY OSBORNE & LITTLE.

GIN

⍙ Pamplemousse

Ice
- 1 ounce London dry gin
- ½ ounce St-Germain elderflower liqueur
- 1 ounce fresh grapefruit juice
- ½ ounce fresh lemon juice
- 1 large basil leaf, for garnish

Fitzgerald thinks the Pamplemousse makes a terrific brunch cocktail: "It's bright, refreshing and low in alcohol—a great pick-me-up."

Fill a cocktail shaker with ice. Add all of the remaining ingredients except the garnish and shake well. Pour through a fine strainer into a chilled coupe and garnish with the basil leaf.

▌ Tonic & Gin

Ice
- 1 ounce London dry gin
- 1 ounce Bonal Gentiane-Quina (lightly bitter aperitif wine)
- ½ ounce Cointreau or other triple sec
- ½ ounce fresh lemon juice
- Dash of orange bitters
- 1 ounce chilled club soda
- 1 orange twist, for garnish

Despite the name, this drink contains no tonic; it gets tonic's acidic quinine flavor from Bonal, a French aperitif wine that's infused with quinine and other aromatics. If you can't find Bonal (which is newly available in the U.S.), Dubonnet rouge is a fine substitute.

Fill a cocktail shaker with ice. Add all of the remaining ingredients except the club soda and garnish and shake well. Strain into a chilled collins glass, stir in the club soda and garnish with the orange twist.

48

Foghorn Cocktail

¼ ounce absinthe

Ice

2 ounces gin, preferably Plymouth

½ ounce Cocchi Aperitivo Americano or Lillet blanc

½ ounce Cointreau or other triple sec

1 lemon twist, for garnish

For his boozy update of the Corpse Reviver No. 2, Fitzgerald changed the proportions and replaced the usual Lillet with Cocchi Americano—a fortified, slightly bitter aperitif wine. Absinthe gives the drink an opalescence reminiscent of San Francisco's fog.

———————◇———————

Rinse a chilled coupe with the absinthe; discard the excess. Fill a pint glass with ice. Add the gin, Cocchi Americano and Cointreau; stir well. Strain into the coupe and garnish with the lemon twist.

Lonsdale

Ice

1½ ounces London dry gin

1 ounce unfiltered apple juice

¾ ounce fresh lemon juice

1½ teaspoons honey mixed with 1½ teaspoons warm water

4 basil leaves

Todd Smith, former bar manager at Bourbon & Branch, created the Lonsdale. "It's the perfect drink for guests who say they don't like gin," says Fitzgerald. "The gin, apple juice, honey and basil all create a flavor that's greater than the sum of its parts."

———————◇———————

Fill a cocktail shaker with ice. Add all of the remaining ingredients except 1 basil leaf; shake well. Fine strain into a chilled coupe and garnish with the remaining basil leaf.

GIN

▌ Jasmine Gin Fizz

JASMINE GIN
TIME: 1 HR INFUSING
- 8 ounces gin
- 2 jasmine tea bags

COCKTAIL
- 2 ounces Jasmine Gin
- 1 ounce fresh lemon juice
- 2 teaspoons honey mixed with 2 teaspoons warm water
- 1 large egg white

Ice
- 1 ounce chilled club soda

Jasmine flowers or 3 thin lemon wedges skewered on a pick, for garnish (optional)

Fitzgerald always wanted to incorporate the floral scent of jasmine tea into a cocktail. He chose to add it to the late-19th-century Silver Fizz by using gin infused with jasmine tea.

◇

1 MAKE THE JASMINE GIN In a jar, combine the gin with the tea bags. Let stand for 1 hour. Discard the tea bags. (Leftover infused gin can be kept at room temperature for up to 1 month.)
2 MAKE THE COCKTAIL In a cocktail shaker, combine the 2 ounces of Jasmine Gin with the lemon juice, honey syrup and egg white and shake well. Add ice and shake again. Pour through a fine strainer into a chilled fizz glass, stir in the club soda and garnish with jasmine flowers or skewered lemon wedges.

Jasmine Gin Fizz

*"Kikatsu" stem glass
from ABC Carpet & Home.*

GIN

 ## California Collins

8 fresh lemon verbena leaves or one 1½-inch piece of lemongrass, tender inner white bulb only, crushed

Ice

2 ounces gin, preferably Junípero

2 ounces unfiltered apple juice

1 ounce chilled club soda

Fitzgerald created this drink for the 2009 San Francisco Slow Food Festival using only local ingredients: The gin came from Distillery No. 209 (located at Pier 50 on Fisherman's Wharf), the apples for the juice from a Sonoma orchard and the lemon verbena from an urban garden run by his cousin. Even the club soda was Bay Area–made, by the bottle-recycling Seltzer Sisters.

───────◇───────

In a collins glass, gently muddle the lemon verbena leaves or lemongrass bulb. Add ice and the gin and apple juice; stir well. If using lemongrass, discard the bulb. Stir in the club soda.

 ## Star Ruby

HIBISCUS GIN

TIME: OVERNIGHT INFUSING

- 8 ounces gin
- 1½ tablespoons dried hibiscus flowers or loose hibiscus tea

COCKTAIL

Ice
- 1½ ounces Hibiscus Gin
- 1 ounce Lillet blanc
- ½ ounce Bénédictine (brandy-based herbal liqueur)

While shopping at a Mexican market around the corner from Bourbon & Branch, Fitzgerald picked up some dried hibiscus with the idea of infusing it into a spirit. He opted for gin, knowing the hibiscus would lend a vibrant color but only subtle floral flavors. As he intended, the cocktail is light, complex and delicately floral.

1 MAKE THE HIBISCUS GIN In a jar, combine the gin with the dried hibiscus flowers. Let stand at room temperature overnight. Strain into a jar. (Leftover infused gin can be kept at room temperature for up to 1 month.)
2 MAKE THE COCKTAIL Fill a pint glass with ice. Add the 1½ ounces of Hibiscus Gin, the Lillet blanc and the Bénédictine and stir well. Strain into a chilled coupe.

GIN

Ginger Rogers

6 to 8 mint leaves, plus
    1 mint sprig for garnish
⅔ ounce Ginger-Pepper
    Syrup (below)
Crushed ice
1½ ounces gin
¾ ounce fresh lemon juice
2 ounces chilled
    ginger ale
1 lemon wheel, for
    garnish (optional)

According to Fitzgerald, this drink—created by mixologists Kathy Flick and Marcovaldo Dionysos—is based on the Favorite Cocktail in Jacques Straub's 1914 book *Drinks*. The updated recipe amps up the Favorite's ginger flavor with an intense syrup infused with fresh ginger and black peppercorns.

In a collins glass, muddle the mint leaves with the Ginger-Pepper Syrup. Add crushed ice, then add the gin and lemon juice. Spin a swizzle stick or bar spoon between your hands to mix the drink. Stir in the ginger ale, then garnish with the mint sprig and lemon wheel.

GINGER-PEPPER SYRUP

Thinly slice a 1-inch piece of ginger. In a small saucepan, combine ½ cup sugar with 6 ounces water, 1 teaspoon whole black peppercorns and the ginger. Bring to a simmer over moderate heat, stirring until the sugar dissolves. Cook over low heat for 10 minutes. Remove from the heat; let cool. Strain into a jar, cover and refrigerate for up to 2 weeks. Makes about 8 ounces.

Ginger Rogers

*"18th Century–Inspired" glass
by BollenGlass from John Derian.*

GIN

♈ New Milano

Ice
- 1 ounce London dry gin
- 1 ounce Dimmi (herbal Italian liqueur)
- 1 ounce Cynar

Pinch of salt
- 1 small grapefruit wedge, for garnish

Fitzgerald based this recipe on the Negroni, replacing the Campari with artichoke-flavored Cynar and the sweet vermouth with fruity Dimmi. He also adds salt. "A few bartenders are playing with salt in cocktails," he says. "It helps enhance flavors while counteracting the bitterness in some spirits."

———◇———

Fill a pint glass with ice. Add the gin, Dimmi, Cynar and salt and stir well. Strain into a chilled coupe or wineglass and garnish with the grapefruit wedge.

♈ Youngstown Tube

- ¼ ounce Fernet-Branca (bitter Italian digestif)

Ice
- 1½ ounces London dry gin
- ½ ounce yellow Chartreuse
- ½ ounce apricot liqueur
- ¾ ounce fresh lime juice
- ¼ ounce agave nectar

To commemorate his 2008 guest-bartending stint at Drink in Boston, Fitzgerald concocted this aromatic cocktail. He wanted to include a dash of flavor from his hometown San Francisco in the mix, so he rinsed the glass with Fernet-Branca, the city's unofficial favorite spirit. "It adds a nice saffron aroma."

———◇———

Rinse a coupe with the Fernet-Branca; discard the excess. Fill a cocktail shaker with ice. Add the remaining ingredients and shake well. Fine strain into the coupe.

New Milano

"Essence" sweet wine glass by Iittala.

GIN

♟ Dempsey

Ice
1½ ounces London dry gin
1½ ounces Calvados
 2 dashes of absinthe
 2 teaspoons grenadine,
   preferably homemade
   (p. 18)

"I love the way the Calvados and gin work together," says Fitzgerald of the unlikely combination of spirits in this early-1900s cocktail. His version plays up the apple brandy's flavors and the gin's piney scent.

———————◇———————

Fill a pint glass with ice. Add all of the remaining ingredients and stir well. Strain into a chilled coupe.

♟ Martinez

Ice
1½ ounces Old Tom gin,
   preferably Ransom
 ¾ ounce sweet vermouth
 1 teaspoon maraschino
   liqueur
Dash of Angostura bitters
Dash of orange bitters
 1 lemon twist, for garnish

Most cocktail historians agree that the auburn-colored Martinez, made with sweet vermouth and slightly sweet Old Tom gin, was the precursor to the dry gin martini.

———————◇———————

Fill a pint glass with ice. Add all of the remaining ingredients except the garnish and stir well. Strain into a chilled coupe and garnish with the lemon twist.

GIN

 ## Union League

Ice, plus 2 cubes, preferably
    large
1 ounce Old Tom gin,
    preferably Ransom
1 ounce tawny port
2 dashes of orange
    bitters

A huge fan of Ransom Old Tom gin, which is spicier and less sweet than typical Old Toms, Fitzgerald mixed it with an equal amount of tawny port and decided the drink was terrific. Then he found the same combo in a vintage bar book but with orange bitters and different proportions. He added the bitters, kept his proportions and borrowed the name.

Fill a pint glass with ice. Add the gin, port and bitters and stir well. Strain into a double rocks glass and add 2 ice cubes.

 ## Half-Moon Cocktail

Ice
1½ ounces genever,
    preferably Bols
¾ ounce fresh lemon juice
¾ ounce pineapple gum
    syrup (thickened
    pineapple-flavored
    simple syrup)
2 green cardamom pods
1½ ounces Prosecco or
    other sparkling wine
Dash of Angostura bitters

Genever is a clear distilled spirit from Holland that's typically made from a mixture of malted grains flavored with juniper (the key flavoring in gin). It's often compared to good single-malt whiskey. Pineapple gum syrup is available at smallhandfoods.com.

Fill a cocktail shaker with ice. Add the genever, lemon juice, gum syrup and cardamom pods and shake well. Strain into a chilled coupe and stir in the Prosecco and bitters.

LEFT TO RIGHT: Nicosia, P. 75; Last-Straw Cobbler, P. 72

"Divine" Champagne coupe by Orrefors; "Caroline" wineglass by William Yeoward.

TEQUILA

———————————— ◎ ————————————

PHILIP WARD

Philip Ward's fixation with the agave-based spirits tequila and mezcal began while he was working at New York City's Flatiron Lounge almost ten years ago. "I learned to bartend from classics expert Julie Reiner and old cocktail books. Those books have very few tequila drinks and pretty much no mention of mezcal." Excited to create cocktail history, Ward has been experimenting with those spirits ever since, first at the übercool Death & Co. and, beginning in 2009, at his own tequila and mezcal bar, Mayahuel.

 # Paloma

1	lime wedge and kosher salt (optional)
Ice	
2	ounces blanco tequila
1	ounce fresh grapefruit juice
¾	ounce fresh lime juice
½	ounce Simple Syrup (p. 18)
1	ounce chilled club soda
1	lime wedge, for garnish

This is Ward's take on what might be Mexico's most popular tequila drink. Instead of using bottled grapefruit soda, he combines grapefruit juice, simple syrup and club soda.

———————————— ◎ ————————————

Moisten the outer rim of a highball glass with a lime wedge and coat lightly with salt. Fill the glass with ice. Fill a cocktail shaker with ice, then add the tequila, grapefruit and lime juices and Simple Syrup; shake well. Strain into the glass, stir in the club soda and garnish with a lime wedge.

Paloma

"Hotto" highball glass by Orrefors.

MODE "DARCY" WALLPAPER BY GRAHAM & BROWN.

TEQUILA

▼ Margarita

2 lime wedges and
   kosher salt
Ice
2 ounces blanco tequila
1 ounce Cointreau or
   other triple sec
¾ ounce fresh lime juice

Daisies—consisting of a base spirit, orange liqueur, citrus and sometimes a splash of soda—are thought to have been created in the mid-1800s. "A margarita," says Ward, "is a daisy made with tequila and triple sec."

Moisten the outer rim of a coupe with a lime wedge; coat lightly with salt. Fill a cocktail shaker with ice, then add the tequila, Cointreau and lime juice; shake well. Strain into the coupe and garnish with the remaining lime wedge.

▼ Lipspin

Ice
1½ ounces blanco tequila
¾ ounce Cynar
   (bitter artichoke
   liqueur)
¾ ounce sloe gin
1 brandied cherry, for
   garnish

"The three ingredients in this drink look odd together on paper but are in fact delicious," says Ward. "Cynar is bitter and sloe gin is a bit sweet. I can remember thinking, 'Would they work with tequila?'" They do.

Fill a pint glass with ice. Add the tequila, Cynar and sloe gin and stir well. Strain into a chilled coupe and garnish with the brandied cherry.

🍸 Cinder

JALAPEÑO TEQUILA

TIME: 30 MIN INFUSING

- 5 ounces blanco tequila
- 1 jalapeño, halved and seeded

COCKTAIL

- 1 lime wedge and smoked salt

Ice

- ¾ ounce reposado tequila
- ¾ ounce Jalapeño Tequila
- ½ ounce mezcal
- ¾ ounce fresh lime juice
- ¾ ounce Simple Syrup (p. 18)
- 3 dashes of Angostura bitters

Ward buys smoked salt for the Cinder from New York City's La Boîte á Epice (laboiteny.com). The salt's flavor is intense, so he blends it with two parts kosher salt before using.

———————————— ◎ ————————————

1 MAKE THE JALAPEÑO TEQUILA In a jar, combine the blanco tequila with the jalapeño. Let stand for 30 minutes. Discard the jalapeño. (Leftover infused tequila can be kept at room temperature for up to 1 month.)

2 MAKE THE COCKTAIL Moisten the outer rim of a coupe with the lime wedge and coat lightly with smoked salt. Fill a cocktail shaker with ice. Add the reposado tequila, the ¾ ounce of Jalapeño Tequila and the mezcal, lime juice, Simple Syrup and bitters; shake well. Strain the cocktail into the prepared coupe.

TEQUILA

 ## Dahlgren

Ice
- 2 ounces blanco tequila
- 1 ounce tawny port
- ¾ ounce fresh lime juice
- ½ ounce Simple Ginger Syrup (below)

Dash of Angostura bitters
- 1 ounce chilled club soda
- 4 small pieces of candied ginger skewered on a pick and 1 lime wheel, for garnish

A classic drink called El Diablo (tequila, lime juice, crème de cassis and ginger ale) inspired Ward's Dahlgren. He replaced the ginger ale with club soda and ginger syrup—it has more zing—and the cassis with tawny port.

Fill a cocktail shaker with ice. Add the tequila, port, lime juice, Simple Ginger Syrup and bitters and shake well. Strain into an ice-filled highball glass and stir in the club soda. Garnish with the candied ginger and lime wheel.

SIMPLE GINGER SYRUP

Coarsely chop three 3-inch pieces of fresh ginger. In a mini processor, puree the ginger. Press the puree through a fine strainer; you should have about 1 ounce of juice. Return the juice to the processor and add 6 tablespoons superfine sugar; process until well mixed. Strain the syrup into a jar, cover and refrigerate for up to 1 week. Makes about 1½ ounces.

Dahlgren

"Coro Gold" highball glass by LSA from the Conran Shop.

TEQUILA

🍸 Silver Monk

2 cucumber slices,
  plus 1 cucumber spear
  for garnish
8 mint leaves
Pinch of salt
½ ounce Simple
  Syrup (p. 18)
Ice
2 ounces blanco tequila
¾ ounce yellow
  Chartreuse
1 ounce fresh lime juice

"I worship Chartreuse," says Ward of the spicy French herbal liqueur. While working as head bartender at New York City's Pegu Club, he invented a drink by combining Chartreuse with tequila. Cocktail enthusiast John Deragon, who was one of the first people to taste the drink, coined its name: Silver (a.k.a. blanco) for the type of tequila, Monk for the Carthusian monastics who make Chartreuse.

In a cocktail shaker, muddle the cucumber slices, 7 of the mint leaves and the salt in the Simple Syrup. Add ice and the tequila, Chartreuse and lime juice and shake well. Pour through a fine strainer into a chilled coupe and garnish with the cucumber spear and the remaining mint leaf.

68

Silver Monk

*"Patrician" finger bowl by
Josef Hoffmann for
Lobmeyr from Neue Galerie.*

TEQUILA

■ Oaxaca Old-Fashioned

Ice
1½ ounces reposado
tequila
½ ounce mezcal
2 dashes of Angostura
bitters
1 teaspoon agave nectar
1 orange twist, flamed
(p. 16), for garnish

"This was one of the first cocktails I made using mezcal; I realized that combining mezcal with tequila was like putting tequila on steroids," says Ward. "Most tequila in the U.S. is only 80 proof, and I wanted more oomph! I discovered the oomph in mezcal."

Fill a pint glass with ice. Add all of the remaining ingredients except the garnish and stir well. Strain into an ice-filled double rocks glass and garnish with the flamed orange twist.

▼ Broxburn

1 lime wedge and kosher
salt
Ice
1½ ounces reposado
tequila
1 ounce Drambuie
(honey-flavored
liqueur)
½ ounce mezcal
¾ ounce fresh lime juice

"I really like the Broxburn's complexity," says Ward of this margarita variation. "The mezcal adds smoke and the Drambuie adds an herbaceous, Scotch-like depth, yet it remains a very refreshing cocktail."

Moisten the outer rim of a coupe with the lime wedge and coat lightly with salt. Fill a cocktail shaker with ice, then add all of the remaining ingredients and shake well. Strain into the prepared coupe.

TEQUILA

■ Suro-Mago

¼ ounce mezcal
Ice
2 ounces reposado
   tequila
¾ ounce manzanilla
   sherry
½ ounce St-Germain
   elderflower liqueur
Dash of orange bitters
1 grapefruit twist, for
   garnish

Ward named the bright, citrusy Suro-Mago after tequila advocate David Suro-Piñera, who owns Tequilas Restaurant in Philadelphia and makes the Siembra Azul tequila that Ward uses in the drink.

Rinse a chilled double rocks glass with the mezcal; discard the excess. Fill a pint glass with ice. Add all of the remaining ingredients except the twist and stir well. Strain into the prepared glass, pinch the twist over the drink and discard the twist.

■ R'Cobbler

1 grapefruit twist
1 sugar cube
½ ounce Campari
2 ounces reposado
   tequila
½ ounce Punt e Mes
   (spicy sweet vermouth)
½ ounce Carpano Antica
   Formula or other sweet
   vermouth
Dash of mole bitters
Crushed ice
1 orange twist, for garnish

Says Ward of the R'Cobbler, "I am a Campari-holic and I also love grapefruit twists and mole bitters (available at bittermens.com). This drink is my trifecta."

In a cocktail shaker, muddle the grapefruit twist and sugar cube with the Campari. Add the tequila, both vermouths and the bitters and shake well. Pour into a double rocks glass, add crushed ice and garnish with the orange twist.

TEQUILA

■ Last-Straw Cobbler

2 strawberries, quartered,
   plus 1 strawberry
   for garnish
½ ounce Velvet Falernum
   (clove-spiced liqueur)
2 ounces añejo tequila
Dash of Fee Brothers
   Whiskey Barrel–Aged
   bitters or Angostura
   bitters
Crushed ice

The first cobblers, thought to have been invented in the 1830s, consisted of sherry, sugar, fruit and lots of shaved ice. Ice remains the hallmark of a good cobbler, even high-proof versions like this one (which, Ward advises, should be served with a wide straw).

In a cocktail shaker, muddle the quartered strawberries in the falernum. Add the tequila and bitters; shake well. Pour into a double rocks glass or wineglass, top with crushed ice and garnish with a strawberry.

♈ Division Bell

Ice
1 ounce mezcal
¾ ounce Aperol (bitter
   orange Italian aperitif)
½ ounce maraschino
   liqueur
¾ ounce fresh lime juice
1 grapefruit twist,
   preferably spiral-cut
   (p. 16), for garnish

This drink was one of the 20 tequila and mezcal cocktails on Mayahuel's opening menu (there are now about 45 on the list). The name references the Pink Floyd album that Ward listened to over and over while constructing the bar.

Fill a cocktail shaker with ice. Add all of the remaining ingredients except the garnish and shake well. Strain into a chilled coupe or martini glass and garnish with the grapefruit twist.

Division Bell

*"Pulse" martini glass
by Calvin Klein Home.*

TEQUILA

◼ Barrio Viejo

½ teaspoon absinthe
½ teaspoon mezcal
Ice
2 ounces añejo tequila
1 teaspoon cane syrup or Rich Simple Syrup (p. 18)
2 dashes of Angostura bitters
2 dashes of Peychaud's bitters
1 orange twist, for garnish

Instead of using simple syrup in the Barrio Viejo, Ward opts for cane syrup (available at cocktailkingdom.com). He says, "For this drink, I wanted the extra richness that cane syrup provides. The three sweeteners I use most often, in increasing amounts of richness, are simple syrup, cane syrup and amber agave nectar. I think of them as small, medium and large."

Rinse a chilled double rocks glass with the absinthe and mezcal; discard the excess. Fill a pint glass with ice. Add the tequila, cane syrup and both bitters and stir well. Strain into the prepared double rocks glass. Pinch the orange twist over the drink and discard the twist.

🍸 17ᵗʰ Century

Ice
1½ ounces mezcal
¾ ounce Lillet blanc
¾ ounce white crème de cacao
¾ ounce fresh lemon juice

According to Ward, two of the things Oaxaca, Mexico, is famous for are mezcal (produced there since the 17th century and possibly earlier) and chocolate (used in mole sauce). "People have been consuming mezcal and chocolate together for hundreds of years—and for good reason. So it seemed like a no-brainer to combine them in a cocktail."

———————◎———————

Fill a cocktail shaker with ice. Add all of the remaining ingredients and shake well. Strain into a chilled coupe.

🍸 Nicosia

Ice
1 ounce mezcal
¾ ounce tawny port
¾ ounce Amaro Lucano

Amaro Lucano is a slightly bitter herbal Italian liqueur that Ward says tastes a bit like chocolate. Combined with rich tawny port and smoky mezcal, it's a terrific digestif.

———————◎———————

Fill a pint glass with ice. Add the mezcal, tawny port and amaro and stir well. Strain into a chilled coupe.

RUM

Stepping Razor Blade, P. 81

*"Pythagore" Champagne saucers in amber
and clear by J.L. Coquet from DeVine Corporation.*

RICHARD BOCCATO

Richard Boccato's love for rum began in the Caribbean: His parents live on St. Lucia, and he's been visiting the island for 20 years. He learned more about the spirit—and about classic drinks made with it—while working alongside Sasha Petraske and Joseph Schwartz at New York City's Little Branch and Milk & Honey. In 2009, he opened Dutch Kills, in Queens, followed by the Manhattan tiki bar Painkiller (where rum is the focus). His latest project is Weather Up Tribeca, a classics-driven cocktails spot.

■ Louanalao

1	strawberry, quartered
Ice	
1½	ounces white rum
½	ounce Campari
¼	ounce St. Elizabeth Allspice Dram (rum-based allspice liqueur)
1	ounce fresh lime juice
½	ounce cane syrup or Rich Simple Syrup (p. 18)
1	orange wheel and 1 strawberry, for garnish

Boccato dubbed this tropical drink after the ancestral name for St. Lucia, where his parents run a B&B. He prefers making the cocktail with Chairman's Reserve Silver (a.k.a. white) rum because it's one of the best he's ever tasted—and it's made on St. Lucia.

In a cocktail shaker, muddle the quartered strawberry. Add ice and the remaining ingredients except the garnishes; shake well. Strain into an ice-filled double rocks glass. Garnish with the fruit.

Louanalao

*"Bar" double old-fashioned
glass by Moser.*

ORNAMENTA "VICE VERSA" WALLPAPER BY STARK WALLCOVERING.

RUM

 Air Mail

Ice
1 ounce white rum
½ ounce fresh lime juice
2 teaspoons honey mixed
    with 1 teaspoon warm
    water
1 ounce chilled
    Champagne

This is an adaptation of the Air Mail cocktail in W. C. Whitfield's 1941 *Here's How,* which calls for "a jigger of fine rum" in addition to lime juice, honey and Champagne. Boccato opts for white rum but says aged rum is tasty, too.

Fill a cocktail shaker with ice. Add the rum, lime juice and honey syrup and shake well. Strain into a chilled coupe and stir in the Champagne.

Chicago Fizz

1 ounce white rum
1 ounce tawny port
¾ ounce fresh lemon juice
½ ounce Simple Syrup
    (p. 18)
1 large egg white
Ice
½ ounce chilled club soda
1 orange slice, for
    garnish

Boccato based his Chicago Fizz on the one in Jacques Straub's 1914 *Drinks.* In addition to having a smooth and silky texture, cocktails shaken with egg whites are alleged to cure (or at least lessen) hangovers.

In a cocktail shaker, combine the rum, port, lemon juice, Simple Syrup and egg white and shake well. Add ice and shake again. Strain the drink into a chilled fizz glass, stir in the club soda and garnish with the orange slice.

♈ Stepping Razor Blade

Ice
- 2 ounces Jamaican rum
- ¾ ounce fresh lemon juice
- ½ ounce orgeat (almond-flavored syrup)
- Pinch of cayenne pepper, for garnish

The Stepping Razor Blade fuses two old-time cocktails into one rum drink: the Holland Razor Blade (gin, lemon juice and cayenne pepper) and the Army & Navy (gin, lemon juice and orgeat).

———————◇———————

Fill a cocktail shaker with ice. Add the rum, lemon juice and orgeat and shake well. Strain into a chilled coupe and garnish with the cayenne.

♈ Wildflower

Ice
- 1 ounce aged rhum agricole
- 1 ounce Cognac
- 1 ounce fresh lime juice
- ½ ounce pure maple syrup
- 1 orange wedge
- Pinch of cinnamon, for garnish

This drink was inspired by one called Night Flight in the 1947 *Bartender's Guide by Trader Vic*. That recipe combined fresh lime juice, maple syrup and rhum agricole. Boccato added Cognac, an orange wedge and cinnamon.

———————◇———————

Fill a cocktail shaker with ice. Add the rhum agricole, Cognac, lime juice, maple syrup and orange wedge and shake well. Strain into a chilled coupe and garnish with the cinnamon.

RUM

 ## Cradle of Life

¾ ounce white rum
¾ ounce spiced rum
½ ounce orgeat
⅓ ounce fresh lemon juice
⅓ ounce fresh lime juice
⅓ ounce fresh orange juice
2 dashes of Angostura bitters
Crushed ice
1 hollowed-out lime half, for garnish
½ ounce green Chartreuse

Bartender and Dutch Kills co-owner Karin Stanley came up with this citrusy cocktail. The flamed Chartreuse in the lime cup is poured into the drink once the fire is blown out.

In a cocktail shaker, combine the rums, orgeat, citrus juices and bitters; shake well. Pour into a chilled double rocks glass. Add crushed ice and garnish with the lime cup. Pour the Chartreuse into the cup and ignite the Chartreuse. Blow out the flame before drinking.

 ## Don Gorgon

Ice
1½ ounces aged cachaça
½ ounce Aperol
1 ounce fresh lime juice
½ ounce Rich Simple Syrup (p. 18)
1 ounce chilled club soda
1 cinnamon stick and 1 lime wedge, for garnish

When Boccato received a bottle of aged Cabana cachaça to experiment with, he fell in love with "its almost Cognac-like characteristics." He combined it with Aperol, a bitter orange Italian liqueur, and came up with this great cool-weather cocktail.

Fill a cocktail shaker with ice. Add the cachaça, Aperol, lime juice and Rich Simple Syrup; shake well. Strain into an ice-filled collins glass, stir in the club soda and garnish with the cinnamon and lime.

Cradle of Life

"Meadow" tumbler by William Yeoward.

RUM

 ## Hotel Nacional

Ice
- 2 ounces añejo rum
- ¼ ounce apricot liqueur
- 1 ounce pineapple juice
- ½ ounce fresh lime juice
- ½ ounce Simple Syrup (p. 18)
- 1 pineapple slice or lime wedge, for garnish

According to A. S. Crockett's 1935 *Old Waldorf-Astoria Bar Book,* the National Cocktail was one of the signature drinks at Havana's Hotel Nacional de Cuba. Boccato's version switches in smooth añejo rum for the National's white rum, uses lime juice instead of lemon and adds simple syrup.

———————⬦———————

Fill a cocktail shaker with ice. Add all of the remaining ingredients except the garnish; shake well. Strain into a chilled martini glass; garnish with the pineapple.

 ## Stay Up Later

Ice
- 1½ ounces añejo rum
- ½ ounce pisco
- ¾ ounce fresh lemon juice
- ¾ ounce Simple Syrup (p. 18)
- 1 ounce chilled club soda
- ¼ ounce mezcal
- 1 orange wedge and 1 cherry, for garnish

In this variation on the Stay Up Late cocktail from Lucius Beebe's 1946 *Stork Club Bar Book,* Boccato replaces the original drink's gin and Cognac with pisco, mezcal and añejo rum. (He likes Diplomático rum for its deep molasses flavor and reasonable price.)

———————⬦———————

Fill a cocktail shaker with ice. Add the rum, pisco, lemon juice and syrup; shake well. Strain into a chilled highball glass, stir in the soda and float the mezcal on top. Garnish with the orange and cherry.

Hotel Nacional

"Casanova" martini glass by Moser.

RUM

♈ Via Vero

2 ounces añejo rum
½ ounce pear liqueur
½ ounce Carpano Antica Formula or other sweet vermouth
2 dashes of Jerry Thomas' Own Decanter bitters
1 lemon twist, for garnish

Boccato and bartender Zachary Gelnaw-Rubin came up with the Via Vero ("truthful way") as a kind of rum-based Manhattan.

———◇———

In a pint glass, combine all of the ingredients except the garnish and stir well. Strain into a chilled coupe and garnish with the lemon twist.

■ Triple A

2 ounces añejo rum
1 ounce fresh lemon juice
½ ounce orgeat (almond-flavored syrup)
Crushed ice
½ ounce dark rum
Freshly grated nutmeg and 1 lemon wedge, for garnish

The Triple A is the brainchild of Abraham Hawkins and Amanda Pumarejo, both bartenders at Dutch Kills, and Anthony Sarnicola, a regular at the bar.

———◇———

In a cocktail shaker, combine the añejo rum, lemon juice and orgeat; shake well. Pour into a chilled double rocks glass. Add crushed ice and the dark rum. Top with more crushed ice to create a tricolor effect. Garnish with the nutmeg and lemon wedge.

Horse Tonic

1½ ounces dark rum,
  preferably Gosling's
  Black Seal
½ ounce dark rum,
  preferably Cruzan
  Black Strap
¼ ounce Velvet Falernum
  (clove-spiced liqueur)
¾ ounce fresh lemon juice
½ ounce Simple Ginger
  Syrup (p. 66)
1 large egg white
Ice
1 ounce chilled club soda
Pinch of ground espresso
  and 1 orange twist,
  for garnish

Boccato invented the Horse Tonic as a hangover remedy in the vein of mid- to late-19th-century "bracers" (invigorating alcoholic drinks) like the Saratoga Brace Up. "This style of drink became popular with the advent of widely available charged [sparkling] water," he says.

In a cocktail shaker, combine the rums, Velvet Falernum, lemon juice, Simple Ginger Syrup and egg white and shake well. Add ice and shake again. Strain into a chilled fizz glass, stir in the club soda and garnish with the espresso. Pinch the orange twist over the drink and drop it in.

RUM

 ## Testa Dura

1 ounce spiced rum
1 ounce añejo rum
½ ounce fresh orange juice
½ ounce cane syrup or Rich Simple Syrup (p. 18)
½ ounce heavy cream
1 large egg yolk
1 cherry, pitted
Ice
Pinch of freshly grated nutmeg, for garnish

This cocktail's aroma and flavor remind Boccato of zabaglione, an Italian dessert sauce made with egg yolks, sugar and sweet wine. His grandmother made it for him when he visited her in Italy.

———————◇———————

In a cocktail shaker, combine all of the ingredients except the cherry, ice and garnish; shake well. Add the cherry and ice and shake again. Strain into a chilled red wine glass; garnish with the nutmeg.

Dominicana

1 ounce heavy cream
¼ ounce Simple Syrup (p. 18)
Ice
1½ ounces añejo rum
1½ ounces coffee liqueur

Sasha Petraske taught Boccato this White Russian variation when Boccato worked for him at Milk & Honey. Boccato makes it with Caffé Lolita coffee liqueur.

———————◇———————

1 In a cocktail shaker, combine the cream, Simple Syrup and 1 ice cube. Shake well to aerate the cream and melt the ice. 2 Fill a pint glass with ice. Add the rum and liqueur; stir well. Strain into a chilled coupe. Spoon the whipped cream on top.

Dominicana

"Davina" Champagne coupe by William Yeoward.

WHISKEY

LEFT TO RIGHT: Dusk Flip, P. 103; Colorado Cooler, P. 94

"Kikatsu" stem glasses from ABC Carpet & Home; "Equinoxe" highball glass by Baccarat; "Hôtel Silver" cocktail shaker from Bergdorf Goodman.

JOHN COLTHARP

"I don't know if I could ever love another spirit like I love whiskey," says John Coltharp. Currently tending bar at the much-lauded Tasting Kitchen in Venice, California, he became obsessed with the spirit while working at L.A.'s Seven Grand whiskey bar. "I was able to sample the widest variety of whiskeys on the West Coast," he says, "from the smokiest single malt to the sweetest bourbon." He's particularly fond of combining whiskey with "fall flavors" like apple and cinnamon.

 ## Cork County Bubbles

Ice
- 1 ounce Irish whiskey
- ¼ ounce yellow Chartreuse
- ½ ounce fresh lemon juice
- 1 teaspoon honey mixed with ½ teaspoon warm water
- 1 ounce chilled Champagne
- 1 lemon twist, preferably spiral-cut (p. 16), for garnish

Coltharp likes making this Champagne cocktail with herbal, woody Jameson 12-year Irish whiskey (made in Ireland's County Cork).

Fill a cocktail shaker with ice. Add all of the remaining ingredients except the Champagne and garnish and shake well. Strain into a chilled flute, stir in the Champagne and garnish with the twist.

Cork County Bubbles

*"Legin" Champagne
flute by Moser.*

"KLASSISK RAND" WALLPAPER BY COUNTRY SWEDISH.

WHISKEY

 ## August Collins

Ice
1½ ounces blended Scotch
1 ounce pear eau-de-vie
1 ounce Simple Syrup
(p. 18)
¾ ounce fresh lemon juice
5 raspberries
2 ounces chilled club
soda

"L.A. is T-shirt-and-shorts weather nine months of the year," says Coltharp, "so you need to know how to make a summer drink that's interesting." This fizzy one features the unlikely combination of Scotch, raspberries and pear eau-de-vie.

———————————|||———————————

Fill a cocktail shaker with ice. Add the Scotch, eau-de-vie, Simple Syrup, lemon juice and 4 raspberries; shake well. Strain into an ice-filled collins glass, stir in the club soda and garnish with a raspberry.

 ## Colorado Cooler

4 cherries, preferably
Rainier, pitted, plus
1 cherry for garnish
Ice
2 ounces malt whiskey,
preferably Stranahan's
Colorado Whiskey
¾ ounce fresh lemon juice
¾ ounce Simple Syrup
(p. 18)
2 dashes of celery bitters
(optional)
1 ounce chilled club soda

Stranahan's Colorado Whiskey is a distinctive small-batch whiskey made in Denver from 100 percent malted barley. The flavor is malty and slightly vanilla-y.

———————————|||———————————

In a cocktail shaker, muddle the 4 pitted cherries. Add ice and all of the remaining ingredients except the club soda and garnish. Shake well. Strain into an ice-filled collins glass, stir in the club soda and garnish with a cherry.

▼ Blind Lemon Jefferson

1 lemon wedge, plus 1 lemon twist for garnish
Ice
2 ounces rye whiskey, preferably Sazerac
4 dashes of Fee Brothers Whiskey Barrel–Aged bitters or Angostura bitters
Scant ¾ ounce fresh lemon juice
¾ ounce Simple Syrup (p. 18)

One night, while Coltharp was devising this drink at Seven Grand, a song by Southern blues musician Blind Lemon Jefferson came on the jukebox. Like the blues, the cocktail combines sadness and joy in the form of sour and sweet.

———————————— ||| ————————————

In a cocktail shaker, lightly muddle the lemon wedge. Add ice and the rye, bitters, lemon juice and Simple Syrup and shake well. Strain into a chilled coupe, pinch the twist over the drink and drop it in.

Presbyterian's Aversion

Ice
2 ounces rye whiskey, preferably Russell's Reserve
½ ounce Averna amaro
¾ ounce fresh lime juice
½ ounce Simple Ginger Syrup (p. 66)
1 ounce chilled club soda
1 lime wedge, for garnish

Coltharp has tried making ginger-and-rye drinks with scores of different *amari* (herbal, bittersweet Italian liqueurs). This version, which uses citrusy Averna amaro, is one of his favorites: "It's great with buttery desserts or stinky cheese."

———————————— ||| ————————————

Fill a cocktail shaker with ice. Add all of the remaining ingredients except the club soda and garnish; shake well. Strain into an ice-filled collins glass, stir in the club soda and garnish with the lime wedge.

WHISKEY

 ## Descanso Beach Smash

4 lemon wedges

5 mint leaves, plus 1 mint sprig for garnish

Ice

2 ounces rye whiskey

¾ ounce Aperol (bitter orange Italian aperitif)

¼ ounce Simple Syrup (p. 18)

3 small orange wedges skewered on a pick, for garnish

While vacationing in 2008 with his wife's family on a boat near Catalina Island, California, Coltharp was dismayed to see that all the beach bars focused on sweet drinks like piña coladas. Back on his father-in-law's boat, he came up with this pleasantly bitter and refreshing concoction—with Aperol from the well-stocked bar.

———————————|||———————————

In a cocktail shaker, muddle the lemon wedges and mint leaves. Add ice and the whiskey, Aperol and Simple Syrup and shake well. Pour through a fine strainer into a double rocks glass or wineglass filled with ice cubes or crushed ice. Garnish with the mint sprig and skewered orange wedges.

96

Descanso Beach Smash

*"88/1 Series" wineglasses
by NasonMoretti.*

WHISKEY

 ## Apples to Oranges

2 slices of English
   cucumber, plus 3 or 4
   thin slices for garnish
Ice
2 ounces bourbon
1 ounce fresh white
   grapefruit juice
½ ounce Simple Syrup
   (p. 18)
Dash of celery bitters
   (optional)

People who taste this citrusy cocktail almost always guess that it contains apples or oranges or some other fruit, but never the actual ingredients: cucumber and grapefruit.

———————————|||———————————

In a cocktail shaker, muddle the 2 cucumber slices. Add ice and all of the remaining ingredients except the garnish and shake well. Strain into an ice-filled double rocks glass and garnish with the thin cucumber slices.

"Top Shelf" Julep

10 mint leaves, plus 2 mint
   sprigs for garnish
¾ ounce Simple Syrup
   (p. 18)
1½ ounces overproof
   bourbon
¾ ounce peach eau-de-vie
Crushed ice
½ ounce aged
   pot still rum

"There are so many great mass-produced liquors available today," says Coltharp. He uses one of them, Old Grand-Dad 114 bourbon, in this julep. "It's inexpensive and packed with flavor."

———————————|||———————————

In a highball glass, muddle the mint leaves with the Simple Syrup, then add the bourbon and eau-de-vie. Add crushed ice and stir, then add more crushed ice to fill the glass. Top with the rum and arrange the mint sprigs in the center of the drink.

98

Apples to Oranges

"Cubism" glass by Moser.

WHISKEY

 The Bobby Boucher

Ice
- 2 ounces overproof bourbon
- ½ ounce Carpano Antica Formula or other sweet vermouth
- ¼ ounce cherry Heering (cherry liqueur)
- ¼ ounce Bénédictine (brandy-based herbal liqueur)
- 1 orange twist, for garnish

This drink is based on the 1930s Bobby Burns. Changing the Scotch in the original to bourbon made the drink Southern; trading some of the vermouth for cherry Heering made it a little sweet, says Coltharp.

———————————— ‖‖ ————————————

Fill a chilled pint glass with ice. Add all of the remaining ingredients except the garnish and stir well. Strain into an ice-filled coupe, pinch the orange twist over the drink and drop it in.

 Seven Sins Cocktail

Ice
- 1 ounce rye whiskey
- 1 ounce applejack
- ¾ ounce fresh lemon juice
- ¾ ounce grenadine, preferably homemade (p. 18)
- 2 dashes of Angostura bitters

Pinch of cinnamon, for garnish

The Jack Rose (applejack, lime juice and grenadine) is one of Coltharp's favorite brandy drinks. Seven Sins is his attempt at converting it into a whiskey cocktail. He strongly recommends preparing your own grenadine: "It makes you wince at the store-bought stuff."

———————————— ‖‖ ————————————

Fill a cocktail shaker with ice. Add all of the remaining ingredients except the garnish and shake well. Strain into a chilled coupe; garnish with the cinnamon.

The Bobby Boucher

"Verve" cocktail glass by Steuben.

WHISKEY

♈ Historic Core Cocktail

Ice
- 1 ounce bonded rye whiskey, such as Rittenhouse
- ¾ ounce bonded apple brandy
- ¾ ounce Carpano Antica Formula or other sweet vermouth
- ¼ ounce green Chartreuse
Dash of Angostura bitters
- 1 lemon twist, for garnish (optional)

Coltharp created this drink for a 2008 contest held by L.A. bartender Marcos Tello. All entries had to be named after sub-districts in the city's downtown. The Historic Core Cocktail, made with rye and apple brandy, honors the area where Coltharp lived then.

———————— ‖‖ ————————

Fill a pint glass with ice. Add all of the remaining ingredients except the garnish and stir well. Strain into a chilled coupe, pinch the lemon twist over the drink and drop it in.

♈ Blackened Orange

- ¼ ounce smoky single-malt Scotch, such as Islay
Ice
- 2 ounces rye whiskey
- ½ ounce Campari
- ½ ounce Amaro Nonino or other amaro (Italian herbal liqueur)
- 2 dashes of orange bitters
- 1 orange twist, flamed (p. 16), for garnish

Longtime Seven Grand bartender Leo Rivas came up with the Blackened Orange, which Coltharp describes as super-intense. Amaro Nonino gives the drink a rich bitter-orange flavor, plus hints of licorice and herbs.

———————— ‖‖ ————————

Rinse a chilled coupe with the Scotch; discard the excess. Fill a pint glass with ice. Add all of the remaining ingredients except the garnish and stir well. Strain into the prepared coupe and garnish with the flamed twist.

102

WHISKEY

♟ The Dana Barrett

Ice
- 1   ounce single-malt rye whiskey, preferably Old Potrero 18th Century Style Whiskey
- 1   ounce Amaro Nonino or other amaro
- 1   ounce Dolin Blanc or other bianco vermouth
- ½   ounce fresh lime juice

Dash of Jerry Thomas' Own Decanter bitters (optional)

Old Potrero 18th Century emulates the style of early American high-proof whiskeys: It's made with 100 percent rye malt in a small copper pot still. (To find Jerry Thomas' Own Decanter bitters, go to the-bitter-truth.com.)

———— ‖ ————

Fill a cocktail shaker with ice. Add all of the remaining ingredients and shake well. Strain into a chilled coupe.

♟ Dusk Flip

- 3   blackberries, plus 1 blackberry skewered on a pick for garnish
- 2   ounces Irish whiskey
- 1   large egg
- ½   ounce heavy cream
- ½   ounce Simple Syrup (p. 18)

Ice

Small pinch of freshly grated nutmeg, for garnish

"This is the drink I would choose instead of dessert after a big meal," says Coltharp. Fruity, spicy Redbreast Irish whiskey is excellent with the blackberries.

———— ‖ ————

In a cocktail shaker, muddle the 3 berries. Add the whiskey, egg, cream and Simple Syrup; shake well. Add ice and shake again. Pour through a fine strainer into a chilled coupe and garnish with the skewered berry and nutmeg.

BRANDY

Corpse Reviver No. 1, P. 115

"Culbuto" decanter by Moser; "Juwel" Champagne coupe by Theresienthal from TableArt; "Hostess" brass dish by Kelly Wearstler for Bergdorf Goodman.

JACKSON CANNON

During his dozen years of bartending, Jackson Cannon has developed a preference for brandy drinks. "There's so much variety," he says, referring to Cognac, Armagnac, Calvados and eaux-de-vie—all brandies. Currently the bar director for Eastern Standard and Island Creek Oyster Bar, both in Boston, Cannon even created a limited-edition Cognac blend in 2010 with longtime producer Alain Royer. Made with spirits that had been hidden since before World War II, it's called the Forgotten Casks Lot JC1.

Marasca Acida

Ice
1½ ounces kirsch
¾ ounce Aperol (bitter orange Italian aperitif)
¾ ounce fresh lemon juice
¼ ounce Simple Syrup (p. 18)
1 spiral-cut orange twist (p. 16), for garnish

Cannon describes the Marasca Acida as a "funky, tart and refreshing aperitif." The kirsch (cherry eau-de-vie) gives it an earthy, fruity flavor and the bright orange, pleasingly bitter Aperol creates its lovely coral color.

Fill a cocktail shaker with ice. Add all of the remaining ingredients except the garnish and shake well. Strain into a chilled coupe or martini glass and garnish with the orange twist.

Marasca Acida

*"Larabee Dot" martini glass
by Kate Spade for Lenox.*

BRANDY

 ## Palisade's Pear Fizz

- 2 ounces pear eau-de-vie
- ½ ounce fresh lemon juice
- ½ ounce Chinese Five-Spice Syrup (below)
- 1 large egg white

Ice

- 2 ounces chilled sparkling water
- 1 lemon twist, for garnish

Sean Kenyon, bar manager at the Squeaky Bean in Denver, created this fizz to showcase Peach Street Distillers' Jack and Jenny pear eau-de-vie (clear fruit brandy). The distillery uses Bartlett pears grown in Palisade, Colorado, a high-elevation spot where the fruit develops an especially high concentration of natural sugars.

In a cocktail shaker, combine the eau-de-vie, lemon juice, Chinese Five-Spice Syrup and egg white and shake well. Add ice and shake again. Strain into a chilled collins glass, then stir in the sparkling water. Pinch the lemon twist over the drink and drop it in.

CHINESE FIVE-SPICE SYRUP

In a small saucepan, bring 4 ounces water to a boil with ¾ cup Demerara or turbinado sugar and 1½ tablespoons Chinese five-spice powder. Lower the heat and simmer for 5 minutes. Cover and let cool, then stir in ¼ ounce rum, preferably Demerara rum. Strain the syrup into a jar, cover and refrigerate for up to 1 month. Makes about 6 ounces.

Cardamomo

1½ ounces grappa
1 ounce Cardamom Syrup (below)
¾ ounce fresh lemon juice
2 dashes of Angostura bitters
1 large egg white
Ice
1 ounce chilled club soda
1 chocolate-dipped candied orange slice and 1 maraschino cherry skewered together on a pick, for garnish (optional)

"I have a cardamom fetish, born of a love for masala tea," says Cannon about what inspired him to devise this great winter cocktail. He uses two parts green cardamom to one part black for the drink's Cardamom Syrup. "The green gives it an intoxicating aroma; the black gives it backbone and earthy, peppery spice."

In a cocktail shaker, combine the grappa, Cardamom Syrup, lemon juice, bitters and egg white and shake well. Add ice and shake again. Strain into an ice-filled pilsner glass. Stir in the club soda and garnish with the candied orange slice and cherry.

CARDAMOM SYRUP

In a spice grinder, coarsely grind 1½ teaspoons cardamom pods. In a small saucepan, combine the ground cardamom with 4 ounces water and bring to a boil. Remove from the heat, cover and let stand for 20 minutes. Fine strain into a jar. Add ½ cup sugar, cover and shake until dissolved. Refrigerate for up to 3 weeks. Makes about 6 ounces.

BRANDY

❗ Belle de Jour

Ice
½ ounce brandy
½ ounce Bénédictine
  (brandy-based herbal
  liqueur)
½ ounce fresh lemon juice
½ ounce grenadine,
  preferably homemade
  (p. 18)
3 ounces chilled
  Champagne
1 lemon twist, for garnish

This sparkling cocktail can easily be made in large batches. Combine equal parts brandy, Bénédictine, lemon juice and grenadine, then bottle and chill. When guests are ready, just pour some of the mixture into flutes and top with Champagne.

Fill a cocktail shaker with ice. Add the brandy, Bénédictine, lemon juice and grenadine and shake lightly. Strain into a chilled flute, stir in the Champagne and garnish with the lemon twist.

■ The Don's Bramble

6 blackberries
½ ounce Simple Syrup
  (p. 18)
¼ ounce fresh lemon juice
Pinch of salt
2 ounces pisco
Crushed ice
1 small edible orchid
  or 1 lemon twist, for
  garnish

Cannon calls this drink a celebration of late summer. He sources the berries from New England farms, including Sparrow Arc Farm in Troy, Maine, and Sylvan Nurseries in Westport, Massachusetts.

In a cocktail shaker, muddle the berries, Simple Syrup, lemon juice and salt. Add the pisco; shake. Fine strain into a chilled double rocks glass, add crushed ice and garnish with an orchid or lemon twist.

The Don's Bramble

"Abysse" tumbler by Baccarat.

BRANDY

■ El Capitán

Ice
- 1 ounce pisco
- 1 ounce Carpano Antica Formula or other sweet vermouth
- ¾ ounce Cynar
- 1½ teaspoons Fernet-Branca (bitter Italian digestif)
- 1 scant teaspoon Créole Shrubb or other orange liqueur
- 1 orange twist, for garnish

El Capitán is a Peruvian interpretation of a Manhattan, featuring the country's indigenous spirit pisco. Cannon augments the recipe with the artichoke-flavored liqueur Cynar, spicy Fernet-Branca and orangey Créole Shrubb.

———————⬡———————

Fill a pint glass with ice. Add the pisco, vermouth, Cynar, Fernet-Branca and Créole Shrubb and stir well. Strain into a chilled double rocks glass and garnish with the orange twist.

BRANDY

◼ French Quarter

1 teaspoon sugar
2 dashes of Peychaud's bitters
2 dashes of Angostura bitters
½ teaspoon club soda
2 ounces VSOP Cognac
1 orange slice
1 brandied cherry
Ice

This fancy old-fashioned is made with Cognac instead of the traditional bourbon or blended whiskey.

In a pint glass, stir the sugar with both bitters and the club soda to a paste. Add the Cognac, orange slice and cherry and stir again. Add ice, stir again and strain into an ice-filled double rocks glass.

◼ Cold Spring Cocktail

Ice
1½ ounces Cognac
¾ ounce pure maple syrup
¾ ounce fresh lemon juice, preferably Meyer lemon juice
Dash of rhubarb bitters (optional)
1 orange twist, for garnish

Cannon created this maple-sweetened cocktail in March, when the maple sap flows in New England. "It's a winter sour that I think of as a harbinger of spring," he says. He sometimes uses a piece of house-made candied rhubarb as a garnish.

Fill a cocktail shaker with ice. Add all of the remaining ingredients except the garnish and shake well. Strain into an ice-filled double rocks glass and garnish with the orange twist.

BRANDY

🍸 The Manhattan Exposition

Ice
- 2 ounces Cognac
- ½ ounce sloe gin
- ½ ounce dry vermouth, preferably Dolin

Dash of Boker's bitters
- 1 orange twist, for garnish

Jennifer Salucci, bartender at Deep Ellum in Boston, uses 19th-century components like sloe gin and Boker's bitters (flavored with cardamom and bitter orange peel): "I wanted to make a Manhattan using only ingredients that were around in the late 1800s, just as Manhattans were getting rolling."

Fill a pint glass with ice. Add the Cognac, sloe gin, vermouth and bitters and stir well. Strain into a chilled coupe and garnish with the orange twist.

■ István

Ice
- 2 ounces VSOP Cognac
- ¾ ounce Zwack
- ½ ounce yellow Chartreuse

Dash of Angostura bitters
Dash of orange bitters
- 1 lemon twist, for garnish

The István comes from Nicole Lebedevitch, one of Cannon's fellow bartenders at Eastern Standard. Zwack, a spicy, herbal Hungarian liqueur, gives the drink flavors of chamomile and burnt orange. "This cocktail is the ideal predinner bracer," says Cannon.

Fill a pint glass with ice. Add all of the remaining ingredients except the garnish and stir well. Strain into a chilled double rocks glass. Pinch the lemon twist over the drink, then discard the twist.

114

BRANDY

♈ Vieux Carré

Ice
- 1 ounce VSOP Cognac
- 1 ounce rye whiskey
- 1 ounce sweet vermouth
- 1 teaspoon Bénédictine (brandy-based herbal liqueur)

Dash of Peychaud's bitters
Dash of Angostura bitters
- 1 lemon twist, for garnish

"I'm jumping in with both feet on the lemon twist versus cherry debate," says Cannon of the garnish on this New Orleans classic. "I have a strong preference for a lemon twist to help balance the cocktail and magnify its flavors. Having said that, some of my dear friends prefer the cherry. I'm always happy to oblige."

Fill a pint glass with ice. Add all of the remaining ingredients except the garnish; stir well. Strain into a chilled coupe and garnish with the twist.

♈ Corpse Reviver No. 1

Ice
- 1 ounce Armagnac
- 1 ounce Calvados
- 1 ounce Carpano Antica Formula or other sweet vermouth
- 1 maraschino cherry, for garnish

"I've long loved this pre-Prohibition classic because of its dark, woody notes of apple and bittersweet wine," says Cannon. He came up with this version—which substitutes Armagnac for the usual brandy and Calvados for the applejack—to please a guest who wanted a more "top-shelf" drink.

Fill a pint glass with ice. Add the Armagnac, Calvados and vermouth and stir well. Strain into a chilled coupe and garnish with the cherry.

BRANDY

Spanish Armada

Ice

2 ounces Spanish brandy

¾ ounce East India sherry

½ ounce Licor 43 (citrus-and-vanilla-flavored Spanish liqueur)

Dash of Angostura bitters

1 orange twist, flamed (p. 16), for garnish

According to Cannon, brandy Manhattan drinkers love this cocktail because it's similar to their standby. Using sherry as well as brandy adds a fermented-caramel flavor, making the Spanish Armada a bit more complex.

Fill a pint glass with ice. Add the brandy, sherry, Licor 43 and bitters and stir well. Strain into a chilled double rocks glass and garnish with the flamed twist.

Café Brûlot Flip

1½ ounces Cognac

¾ ounce coffee liqueur, preferably Galliano Ristretto

½ ounce Grand Marnier

¼ ounce Velvet Falernum (clove-spiced liqueur)

1 large egg

Ice

Dash of Fee Brothers Whiskey Barrel–Aged bitters or Angostura bitters, for garnish

Scott Marshall, principal bartender at Drink in Boston, came up with this rich, spicy after-dinner drink. "I love flips," he says of the category of cocktails that contain a whole raw egg. "The egg adds a velvety creaminess that surprises most people."

In a cocktail shaker, combine all of the ingredients except ice and the bitters; shake well. Add ice and shake again. Strain into a chilled coupe; garnish with the bitters, swirling them decoratively.

Café Brûlot Flip

*"Monique" Champagne glasses
by Astier de Villatte from John Derian.*

PUNCHES

Champagne Holiday Punch, P. 123
"Olivia" tumblers and "Berry" Revere bowl by Juliska.

DAVID WONDRICH

David Wondrich is passionate about punch. "It's the original mixed drink," says the Brooklyn-based cocktail historian, former English professor and author of *Punch: The Delights (and Dangers) of the Flowing Bowl*. Wondrich acquired a fondess for rugged spirits like rum from his American mother and more esoteric ones like *amari* from his Italian father. He also consumed huge doses of P. G. Wodehouse and Raymond Chandler and spent a lot of time in bars, which sealed his future as a cocktail historian.

 Felicitation Punch

MAKES ABOUT 18 DRINKS
Strips of zest from 4 lemons
  6 ounces Irish whiskey
One 1-liter bottle gin
  4 ounces maraschino
     liqueur
 12 ounces fresh lemon
     juice
  3 ounces Rich Simple
     Syrup (p. 18)
1½ liters chilled club soda
Ice, preferably 1 large block
     (p. 17)

In this pleasantly tart punch, Wondrich mixes Irish whiskey with gin to mimic the taste of a richer, older style of gin.

In a punch bowl, muddle the lemon zest with the whiskey. Add the gin and let stand for 2 hours. Stir in the maraschino liqueur, lemon juice and Rich Simple Syrup and refrigerate until chilled, about 2 hours. Just before serving, stir in the club soda and add ice.

120

Felicitation Punch

"Dvorak" tumbler by Armani/Casa;
hand-blown punch bowl from L. Becker Flowers.

"NIMBUS" WALLPAPER BY SCHUMACHER.

PUNCHES

 Sassenach Punch

MAKES ABOUT 18 DRINKS

Strips of zest from 6 large
    lemons
½ cup superfine sugar
4 ounces hot water
½ cup honey
8 ounces fresh lemon
    juice
3 ounces fresh orange
    juice, preferably blood
    orange juice
One 750-ml bottle gin,
    preferably Hendrick's
12 ounces blended Scotch
40 ounces chilled
    club soda
Ice, preferably large cubes
Freshly grated nutmeg,
    for garnish

You can use navel oranges in this smoky,
Scotch-spiked punch, but Wondrich likes
blood orange juice for its deep red color.

———◇———

In a bowl, muddle the lemon zest with
the sugar and let stand for 25 minutes.
Muddle again, then add the hot water
and honey and stir until the sugar and
honey dissolve. Add the lemon juice and
orange juice, then strain the liquid into
a punch bowl and add the gin and Scotch.
Refrigerate until chilled, about 2 hours.
Stir in the club soda, add ice and garnish
with nutmeg.

ANATOMY OF A PUNCH *As a rule, punch recipes are very flexible, consisting
basically of a spirit, citrus juice, sugar, water and spice. Whiskey, Cognac,
overproof rum and tequila (reposado or añejo) are all excellent spirit choices;
unsweetened tart fruit juice (like pomegranate) can stand in for fresh citrus juice.
For sweeteners, Simple Syrup (p. 18), honey and flavored syrups are all terrific.
Seltzer, wine and Champagne all work well for diluting the intense punch base.
Nutmeg is the classic punch spice, but cinnamon and cardamom are lovely, too.*

PUNCHES

 Badminton Cup

MAKES ABOUT 8 DRINKS

Strips of peel from
   ½ cucumber
¼ cup plus 2 tablespoons
   superfine sugar
Pinch of freshly grated
   nutmeg
One 750-ml bottle dry red
   wine, such as Bordeaux
16 ounces chilled
   club soda
Ice, preferably 1 large
   block (p. 17)

This punch was originally served in the
mid-1800s at Badminton House, the Duke
of Beaufort's manor in Gloucestershire,
England, and site of the first badminton
game in the U.K.

In a small punch bowl, combine the
cucumber peel, sugar and nutmeg. Add the
wine and stir until the sugar dissolves.
Refrigerate until chilled, about 2 hours. Stir
in the club soda, then add ice.

 Champagne Holiday Punch

MAKES ABOUT 6 DRINKS

12 ounces genever
 4 ounces Créole Shrubb
 6 ounces fresh lemon
   juice
 4 ounces Rich Simple
   Syrup (p. 18)
Angostura bitters
 4 ounces cold Champagne
 8 ounces cold club soda
Ice, preferably large cubes
Pineapple slices and star
   anise pods, for garnish

Erick Castro, former bar manager at San
Francisco's Rickhouse, created this sparkling
punch. It's terrifically light, but the malted
grain–based genever adds whiskey-like depth.

In a small punch bowl, combine the
genever, Créole Shrubb, lemon juice, Rich
Simple Syrup and 10 dashes of the
bitters and refrigerate until chilled, about
2 hours. Stir in the Champagne and
club soda, add ice and garnish with the
pineapple and star anise.

PUNCHES

 ## Georgian Brandy Punch

MAKES 10 TO 12 DRINKS
Strips of zest from 3 lemons
¾ cup Demerara or other raw sugar
6 ounces fresh lemon juice
One 750-ml bottle VSOP Cognac
32 ounces cold water
Ice, preferably 1 large block (p. 17)
Pinch of freshly grated nutmeg, for garnish

Like a martini, this basic punch is entirely satisfying on its own, but it could also be customized or modified in myriad ways. (See Anatomy of a Punch on p. 122 for ideas.)

————————⬦————————

In a punch bowl, muddle the lemon zest with the sugar. Let stand for 1 to 2 hours. Muddle again, add the lemon juice and stir until the sugar dissolves. Add the Cognac and refrigerate until chilled, about 2 hours. Stir in the water, add ice and garnish with the nutmeg.

 ## Gaelic Punch

MAKES ABOUT 14 DRINKS
Strips of zest from 6 lemons, plus 6 thin lemon slices, each studded with 4 cloves, for garnish
¾ cup Demerara or other raw sugar
40 ounces boiling water
One 750-ml bottle Irish whiskey
Pinch of freshly grated nutmeg, for garnish

For hot punches, young Irish whiskeys work best. Heat intensifies the tannic edge of older whiskeys; young ones stay smooth.

————————⬦————————

In a heatproof bowl, muddle the lemon zest with the sugar. Let stand for 1 to 2 hours. Muddle again, add 8 ounces boiling water and stir until the sugar dissolves. Strain into a warm heatproof bowl and stir in the whiskey. Add the remaining 32 ounces of boiling water and garnish with the studded lemon slices and nutmeg.

Gaelic Punch

"Hotto Cut Lines"
cups by Orrefors.

PUNCHES

 ## The Messenger Punch

MAKES ABOUT 16 DRINKS

- 8 ounces pear liqueur
- 12 ounces fresh lemon juice
- 8 ounces pineapple juice
- 2 ounces orgeat (almond-flavored syrup)
- 1½ ounces Don's Spices #2 (TraderTiki.com) or 1½ ounces Vanilla Spice Syrup (below)
- 16 dashes of Fee Brothers Whiskey Barrel–Aged bitters or Angostura bitters
- One 750-ml bottle bonded apple brandy
- 32 ounces chilled club soda
- Ice, preferably 1 large block (p. 17)

Created by Death & Co. bartender Jason Littrell and cocktail blogger Hal Wolin, this drink was one of nine punches served at a huge event in New York City in May 2010. Wondrich, who was the evening's special guest, chose the Messenger Punch as his favorite.

In a punch bowl, combine the pear liqueur, lemon juice, pineapple juice, orgeat, Don's Spices and bitters. Add the apple brandy and refrigerate until chilled, about 2 hours. Stir in the club soda and add ice.

VANILLA SPICE SYRUP

TIME: 24 HR INFUSING

In a jar, combine 1 split vanilla bean, 5 allspice berries, 1 cup sugar and 8 ounces water. Let stand at room temperature, stirring occasionally, for 24 hours. Strain, cover and refrigerate for up to 2 weeks. Makes about 12 ounces.

126

PUNCHES

 Regent's Punch

MAKES ABOUT 26 DRINKS

Strips of zest from 2 lemons

Strips of zest from
    2 oranges

One-half 1-liter bottle
    VSOP Cognac

10 ounces fresh orange
    juice

 4 ounces fresh lemon
    juice

 ¾ cup superfine sugar

 2 ounces maraschino
    liqueur

32 ounces chilled brewed
    green tea

 4 ounces Pineapple
    Syrup (below right)

 4 ounces Jamaican rum

 4 ounces Batavia-Arrack
    van Oosten

Three 750-ml bottles chilled
    Champagne

Marinated Pineapple (right)

Ice

Only recently available in the United States, Batavia-Arrack van Oosten is a spicy, citrusy Javanese spirit made from sugarcane and fermented red rice.

———————◇———————

In a large jar, combine the citrus zests with the Cognac; let stand at room temperature overnight. Strain the Cognac; discard the zests. In a punch bowl, combine the citrus juices. Stir in the sugar until dissolved. Add the infused Cognac, maraschino liqueur, tea and Pineapple Syrup. Stir in the rum and Batavia-Arrack and refrigerate until chilled, about 2 hours. Add the Champagne, Marinated Pineapple and ice.

PINEAPPLE SYRUP & MARINATED PINEAPPLE
TIME: OVERNIGHT MARINATING

In a saucepan, stir 2 cups Demerara sugar into 8 ounces water. Simmer over low heat, stirring, until the sugar dissolves; let cool. Add 3 cups ½-inch pineapple chunks to the syrup; let stand overnight at room temperature. Strain the syrup, reserving the pineapple. The syrup and marinated pineapple can be refrigerated separately for up to 1 week. Makes about 16 ounces of syrup.

PUNCHES

 ## The Victoria Room Punch Bowl

MAKES ABOUT 8 DRINKS

- 18 ounces aged dark rum
- 4½ ounces fresh lemon juice
- 2½ ounces agave nectar mixed with 2½ ounces warm water
- 24 ounces chilled brewed Earl Grey tea
- Ice, preferably large cubes
- 2 lemons, thinly sliced and seeded, and 8 mint sprigs, for garnish

While on a trip to Australia, Wondrich met rum expert Lee Potter Cavanagh. The young mixologist came up with this tea-based punch at Sydney's Victoria Room, where he teaches punch-making classes.

◈

In a small punch bowl, combine the rum, lemon juice and agave syrup. Add the tea and refrigerate until chilled, about 2 hours. Add ice and garnish with the lemon wheels and mint sprigs.

 ## Tea Punch Turenne

MAKES ABOUT 10 DRINKS

- 1 large lemon, thinly sliced and seeded
- 1 cup Demerara or other raw sugar
- 32 ounces hot strong-brewed black tea, such as Earl Grey
- One 750-ml bottle overproof Jamaican rum

According to Wondrich, 18th-century punches were made with high-proof, intensely flavored rums. To achieve that "authentic" flavor, he uses Smith & Cross, a widely available Jamaican rum.

◈

In a heatproof punch bowl, combine the lemon wheels and sugar. Stir in the tea. Pour the rum over the floating lemon wheels and let stand for 1 minute. Using a long match, carefully ignite the rum. Let the flames subside or blow them out, then stir.

PUNCHES

 ## Coffee Milk Punch

MAKES ABOUT 30 DRINKS
- ½ pound ground coffee (ground for French press)
- 64 ounces whole milk
- 1 cup superfine sugar
- 8 ounces fresh lemon juice
- Two 750-ml bottles white rum
- Two-thirds 750-ml bottle Bénédictine (brandy-based herbal liqueur)
- One-half 750-ml bottle maraschino liqueur
- 1½ teaspoons freshly grated nutmeg
- Ice, preferably 1 large block (p. 17)

Mixologists John Gertsen and Misty Kalkofen of Drink in Boston created this sweet, slightly grainy punch. When the milk curdles, says Wondrich, "it will produce a truly revolting-looking mass." Strain the punch through a very-fine-mesh strainer or, even better, through cheesecloth or a clean white T-shirt. Chill thoroughly before serving as a great, potent after-dinner drink.

1 In a large pitcher, stir the ground coffee with the milk and refrigerate for 24 hours. Pour the coffee milk through a fine strainer into a large saucepan and warm over moderate heat; keep warm.
2 In a large bowl, stir the sugar with the lemon juice until the sugar dissolves. Stir in the rum, Bénédictine, maraschino liqueur and nutmeg. Add the warm milk; the mixture will look curdled. Pour the mixture through a fine strainer into a punch bowl and let cool, then refrigerate until chilled, about 2 hours. Add ice.

LEFT TO RIGHT: Bargoens Buck, P. 136; Ginger's Lost Island, P. 146

Brass dish by Kelly Wearstler for Bergdorf Goodman; "Tortoise" highball glass by Ted Muehling for Steuben; "Cliff" old-fashioned glass by NasonMoretti.

MIXOLOGIST ALL-STARS

JIM MEEHAN

When he's not working at his East Village bar PDT, Jim Meehan spends a lot of time tracking down compelling new cocktails and never-before-seen updates of classic drinks. Aside from choosing the talented mixologists featured throughout this book, he also compiled the following roundup of drinks from amazing bartenders around the country. The deputy editor of *FOOD & WINE Cocktails* since 2007, Meehan is also hard at work on the *PDT Cocktail Book,* out in fall 2011.

Aster Family Sour

Zane Harris • Rob Roy, Seattle

1½ ounces Cynar
  1 ounce fresh lemon juice
  ½ ounce orgeat (almond-flavored syrup)
  1 large egg white
Ice
  2 dashes of Angostura bitters, for garnish

The predominant ingredient in the herbal Italian liqueur Cynar is artichoke, a member of the aster family. While Cynar is traditionally drunk neat or on the rocks as a digestif, Harris uses it as the base for this delicious bittersweet sour.

———————— ✳ ————————

In a cocktail shaker, combine the Cynar, lemon juice, orgeat and egg white and shake well. Add ice and shake again. Strain into a chilled coupe, add the bitters and swirl decoratively.

Aster Family Sour

"Amor Vincit Omnia"
Champagne coupe by Orrefors.

"SPHERICA" WALLPAPER BY SCHUMACHER.

ALL-STARS

Strawberry & Grapefruit Collins

Patricia Richards • Wynn Resorts, Las Vegas

1 strawberry
Ice
1½ ounces grapefruit
vodka
½ ounce St-Germain
elderflower liqueur
¾ ounce fresh lemon juice
¾ ounce Simple Syrup
(p. 18)
2 ounces chilled club soda
1 strawberry slice and
1 spiral-cut lemon twist
(p. 16), for garnish

While creating this variation on a Tom Collins, Richards tried all of the grapefruit vodkas she could find on the market. Finlandia was her favorite.

In a cocktail shaker, muddle the whole strawberry. Add ice and all of the remaining ingredients except the club soda and garnishes and shake well. Strain into an ice-filled collins glass, stir in the club soda and garnish with the strawberry slice and lemon twist.

Seersucker Fizz

Jim Romdall • Vessel, Seattle

1 ounce London dry gin
1 ounce Punt e Mes
(spicy sweet vermouth)
½ ounce apricot liqueur
1 ounce fresh lemon juice
¼ ounce Simple Syrup
(p. 18)
1 large egg white
Ice
2 ounces chilled club
soda
1 orange twist, for
garnish

Romdall first served this summery cocktail to a dapper guest wearing a wonderful suit. The man informed Romdall that it was Seersucker Thursday (a Thursday in mid-June), and Romdall named the drink accordingly.

In a cocktail shaker combine all of the ingredients except ice, the club soda and the garnish; shake well. Add ice and shake again. Pour through a fine strainer into a chilled collins glass, stir in the club soda and garnish with the twist.

Contessa

Chris Hannah • Arnaud's French 75 Bar, New Orleans

Ice

1 ounce Aperol (bitter orange Italian aperitif)

¾ ounce gin, preferably Tanqueray

¼ ounce crème de mûre (blackberry liqueur)

¾ ounce Ruby Red grapefruit juice

2 dashes of orange bitters

2 dashes of Angostura bitters

1 orange twist studded with 3 cloves, for garnish

Hannah's spin on the Negroni was inspired by a character called the Contessa in Tennessee Williams's 1950 novel, *The Roman Spring of Mrs. Stone.* "The Contessa was a terrible swindler and instigator who was obsessed with the Negroni," says Hannah. "I felt she deserved a drink named after her."

Fill a cocktail shaker with ice. Add the Aperol, gin, crème de mûre, grapefruit juice, orange bitters and Angostura bitters and shake well. Strain into a chilled coupe and garnish with the clove-studded orange twist.

ALL-STARS

 ## Bargoens Buck

Lindsay Nader · PDT, Manhattan

Ice

1½ ounces genever, preferably Bols

¾ ounce fresh lemon juice

½ ounce Gran Classico Bitter (bittersweet herbal liqueur)

2 dashes of Angostura bitters

3 ounces chilled ginger ale

1 or 2 orange wheels, for garnish

Bols genever was first produced in Amsterdam in 1664. Nader, who tested all of the drinks for *F&W Cocktails 2011*, created this cocktail as a nod to that era. "Bargoens" refers to a Dutch slang spoken in the 17th century, mainly by thieves and drifters.

Fill a cocktail shaker with ice. Add the genever, lemon juice, Gran Classico and bitters and shake well. Strain into an ice-filled collins glass, stir in the ginger ale and garnish with the orange wheels.

 ## Wonderlust

Jonny Raglin · Comstock Saloon, San Francisco

¼ ounce absinthe

Ice

1 ounce genever, preferably Bols

¾ ounce crème de violette (violet liqueur)

¾ ounce pineapple gum syrup (thickened pineapple-flavored simple syrup)

¾ ounce fresh lemon juice

1 spiral-cut lemon twist (p. 16), for garnish

"I have an affinity for the past," says Raglin. Wonderlust is his tribute to cocktail ingredients that were ubiquitous a century back but rare five years ago. Pineapple gum syrup is available at smallhandfoods.com.

Rinse a chilled coupe with the absinthe; discard the excess. Fill a cocktail shaker with ice. Add all the remaining ingredients except the garnish; shake well. Strain into the coupe; garnish with the lemon twist.

136

Wonderlust

"Essence" glass by Iittala.

ALL-STARS

Agricole Mule
Thad Vogler · Bar Agricole, San Francisco

Ice
- 2 ounces aged rhum agricole
- 1 ounce fresh lime juice
- ¾ ounce Simple Ginger Syrup (p. 66)
- ½ ounce cane syrup or Rich Simple Syrup (p. 18)
- 11 mint leaves
- 2 ounces chilled club soda

"Because agricole rums are made from whole sugarcane instead of the usual molasses, they're very aromatic, even gin-like," says Vogler. Here, he uses rich aged agricole rum in place of the gin in a Gin-Gin Mule.

Fill a cocktail shaker with ice. Add all of the remaining ingredients except the club soda and 1 mint leaf; shake well. Pour through a fine strainer into an ice-filled collins glass, stir in the club soda and garnish with the remaining mint leaf.

Flor de Jerez
Joaquín Simó · Death & Co., Manhattan

Ice
- 1½ ounces amontillado sherry
- ½ ounce Jamaican rum
- ¼ ounce apricot liqueur
- ¾ ounce fresh lemon juice
- ½ ounce cane syrup or Rich Simple Syrup (p. 18)

Dash of Angostura bitters

Although Simó's drink is light and lemony, dry amontillado sherry (made in Jerez, Spain) gives it flavors and aromas of toasted almonds and dried fruit.

Fill a cocktail shaker with ice. Add all of the remaining ingredients and shake well. Strain into a chilled coupe.

Y Appletta

Tobin Ellis · BarMagic, Las Vegas

Ice

1½ ounces cachaça

¼ ounce Averna amaro (bittersweet Italian liqueur)

2 ounces apple cider or unfiltered apple juice

½ ounce orgeat (almond-flavored syrup)

½ ounce lemon juice, preferably Meyer lemon juice

5 sage leaves

Ellis designed this sage-and-lemon-spiked take on an apple martini for Scott Conant's excellent Italian restaurant Scarpetta, in New York City. Instead of vodka, Ellis uses cachaça, a Brazilian sugar cane–based spirit with a complex, herbal flavor.

Fill a cocktail shaker with ice. Add the cachaça, Averna, apple cider, orgeat, lemon juice and 4 of the sage leaves and shake well. Strain the cocktail into a chilled martini glass and garnish with the remaining sage leaf.

ALL-STARS

 ## Bridal Shower

Mike Ryan • Sable Kitchen & Bar, Chicago

Ice
2 ounces vodka
¼ ounce Campari
¾ ounce Rhubarb Syrup (below)
¾ ounce fresh lemon juice
Dash of Fee Brothers Old Fashion bitters or Angostura bitters
1 ounce chilled club soda
2 long, thin slices of rhubarb stalk, for garnish

This cocktail reminds Ryan of the strawberry-rhubarb pies his mother made every spring. He roasts the rhubarb for the drink's syrup to caramelize the edges of the stalks and to accentuate their subtle, earthy bitterness. The syrup can be mixed with club soda for a pretty, nonalcoholic drink.

Fill a cocktail shaker with ice. Add all of the remaining ingredients except the club soda and garnish and shake well. Strain into an ice-filled collins glass and stir in the club soda. Garnish with the rhubarb stalks.

RHUBARB SYRUP
TIME: 1 HR

In a glass baking dish, combine ½ pound chopped rhubarb with 1 cup sugar, 8 ounces water and a pinch of salt. Bake in a preheated 325° oven for 1 hour, stirring every 15 minutes, until the rhubarb is very tender. Let cool, then press through a fine strainer. Refrigerate for up to 1 week. Makes about 12 ounces.

Bridal Shower

*"TAC 02" highball glass
by Rosenthal from Unica Home.*

ALL-STARS

Autumn in New York
Danny Valdez • Cure, New Orleans

Ice
- 1 ounce pear brandy
- ½ ounce fresh lemon juice
- ½ ounce Rich Simple Syrup (p. 18)

Dash of apple cider vinegar
- 2 ounces cava or other sparkling wine
- 1 teaspoon St. Elizabeth Allspice Dram (allspice liqueur), for garnish

Vinegars are showing up in more and more cocktails. Combined with lemon juice, the apple cider vinegar in Valdez's drink is peculiarly delicious with the pear brandy.

Fill a cocktail shaker with ice. Add all of the remaining ingredients except the cava and garnish and shake well. Strain into a chilled coupe, stir in the cava and drizzle with the Allspice Dram.

Spice Bandit
Greg Best • Holeman & Finch Public House, Atlanta

Ice
- 1½ ounces Cognac
- ½ ounce Cointreau or other triple sec
- ½ ounce fresh lime juice
- 1 teaspoon St. Elizabeth Allspice Dram (allspice liqueur)
- 1 ounce chilled lambic, preferably peach
- 1 lemon twist, flamed (p. 16), for garnish

According to Best, his first sip of this spicy Cognac-and-peach-lambic cocktail was so evocative, it "brought about visions of strangely garbed folk drinking around the fire pits of their bandit camps on a cold desert night."

Fill a cocktail shaker with ice. Add all of the remaining ingredients except the lambic and garnish and shake well. Strain into a chilled coupe, stir in the lambic and garnish with the flamed twist.

142

Old Faithful Punch

Gina Chersevani · PS 7's, Washington, DC

MAKES ABOUT 20 DRINKS

One 750-ml bottle bourbon

One-half 750-ml bottle St-Germain elderflower liqueur

1 cup superfine sugar

32 ounces fresh Ruby Red grapefruit juice

20 dashes of grapefruit bitters

20 strips of grapefruit zest

One 750-ml bottle chilled sparkling water

½ cup mint leaves, for garnish

Ice

Grapefruit adds a sweet-tart flavor to this citrusy large-batch version of a mint julep. "We had such a demand for the punch and made it so frequently," says Chersevani, "that the staff started to call it 'Old Faithful.'"

In a large bowl, whisk the bourbon with the elderflower liqueur and sugar until the sugar dissolves completely. Stir in the grapefruit juice, bitters and grapefruit zest and refrigerate until chilled, about 2 hours. Stir in the sparkling water and garnish with the mint leaves. Ladle the punch into ice-filled punch cups.

ALL–STARS

Isle of Islay Swizzle

Julie Reiner · Lani Kai, Manhattan

1½ ounces blended Scotch
½ ounce coconut liqueur
¼ ounce single-malt
   Scotch, preferably Islay
1 teaspoon Velvet
   Falernum (clove-spiced
   liqueur)
½ ounce fresh lemon juice
¼ ounce passion fruit
   juice or nectar
Crushed ice
1 pineapple sage sprig
   (optional), for garnish

Smoky single-malt Scotches are almost never used in tropical drinks, but Reiner was sure that one would taste great with passion fruit juice. At Lani Kai, she garnishes this swizzle with grilled pineapple, to play up the Scotch's smokiness.

In a collins glass, combine all of the ingredients except crushed ice and the garnish. Add crushed ice. Spin a swizzle stick or bar spoon between your hands to mix the drink. Garnish with the sage sprig.

Flaming Heart

Toby Maloney · Bradstreet Craftshouse, Minneapolis

Ice
2 ounces blanco tequila
½ ounce Licor 43
¾ ounce fresh lime juice
½ ounce pineapple juice
¼ ounce Simple Syrup
   (p. 18)
3 dashes of Fee Brothers
   Old Fashion bitters
3 dashes of green
   Tabasco
1 lime wheel, for garnish

"Licor 43 is one of my all-time favorite spirits," says Maloney of the citrus-and-vanilla-flavored liqueur. He mixes it here with pineapple juice and green Tabasco to make "a mini vacation in a glass."

Fill a cocktail shaker with ice. Add all of the remaining ingredients except the garnish and shake well. Strain into a chilled double rocks glass and garnish with the lime wheel.

144

Isle of Islay Swizzle

*"Square" glass from
ABC Carpet & Home.*

ALL-STARS

Ginger's Lost Island
Bryan Dayton · Oak at Fourteenth, Boulder, CO

2   cardamom pods
Ice
1¼ ounces mezcal
1¼ ounces ginger liqueur
½   ounce apple juice
½   ounce fresh lime juice
Pinch of cinnamon
¼   ounce agave nectar
1   apple wedge, cut into
    thin slices and fanned,
    for garnish

Dayton's mixture of cardamom, cinnamon, ginger liqueur and smoky mezcal evokes everything from Mexican food to the flavors of Asia and India.

In a cocktail shaker, lightly crush the cardamom. Add ice and all of the remaining ingredients except the garnish and shake well. Pour through a fine strainer into an ice-filled double rocks glass. Garnish with the apple fan.

The Makeup
Ricky Gomez · Teardrop Lounge, Portland, OR

Ice
2   ounces rye whiskey
½   ounce Averna amaro
    (bittersweet Italian
    liqueur)
½   ounce yellow
    Chartreuse
2   dashes of orange
    bitters
1   orange twist, for
    garnish

This is Gomez's after-dinner take on a Manhattan. "It's a little on the sweet side," he says, "but in this world of mixologists wanting to go bitter and more bitter, why not something slightly sweet?"

Fill a pint glass with ice. Add all of the remaining ingredients except the garnish and stir well. Strain into a chilled coupe and garnish with the orange twist.

146

Puritan's Punch

Bob McCoy • Island Creek Oyster Bar, Boston

Ice
1½ ounces aged rum,
      preferably American
 ¾ ounce Spiced Honey
      Syrup (below)
 ¾ ounce fresh lemon juice
Pinch of freshly grated
      nutmeg, for garnish

The name of McCoy's spiced cold-weather punch honors America's early colonists, many of whom produced molasses-based rum in home stills. McCoy likes making the punch with Berkshire Mountain Distillers' Ragged Mountain rum, from Massachusetts.

Fill a cocktail shaker with ice. Add the rum, Spiced Honey Syrup and lemon juice and shake well. Strain into a chilled coupe and garnish with the nutmeg.

SPICED HONEY SYRUP

In a small saucepan, muddle 4 cardamom pods with 1 large cinnamon stick. Add 5 tablespoons finely chopped fresh ginger, 1 cup clover honey and 8 ounces water. Bring just to a boil, then lower the heat and simmer for 15 minutes, stirring frequently. Let cool. Strain through cheesecloth into a jar. Refrigerate for up to 1 month. Makes about 12 ounces.

Salt Air Margarita, P. 152

*"Patrician" Champagne coupe
for Lobmeyr from Neue Galerie;
"Hôtel Silver" cocktail shaker
from Bergdorf Goodman.*

CHEFS' COCKTAILS

CHEFS' COCKTAILS

Porch Crawler

Frank Falcinelli & Frank Castronovo · Prime Meats, Brooklyn, NY

5 cherries, pitted, plus
   1 cherry for garnish
3 mint leaves, plus 1 mint
   sprig for garnish
1 hot chile, such as
   serrano, halved and
   seeded
Ice
2 ounces white rum
1 ounce fresh lemon juice
1 ounce Simple Syrup
   (p. 18)
2 ounces chilled club soda

Chef-partners Falcinelli and Castronovo and their friend Travis Kauffman concocted this terrifically refreshing cooler one hot summer night with ingredients from Falcinelli's rooftop garden.

In a cocktail shaker, muddle the 5 pitted cherries, mint leaves and chile. Add ice and the rum, lemon juice and Simple Syrup; shake well. Strain into an ice-filled collins glass, stir in the club soda and garnish with a cherry and mint sprig.

Golden State

Barbara Lynch · No. 9 Park, Boston

Ice cubes, plus cracked ice
1½ ounces vodka,
    preferably Hangar One
½ ounce St-Germain
    elderflower liqueur
2 ounces fresh white
    grapefruit juice
1 ounce chilled ginger
   beer
1 grapefruit twist, for
   garnish

The bartenders at Lynch's Boston bar Drink created this citrusy cocktail for her with California-made Hangar One vodka after she returned from a trip to the West Coast. She christened the cocktail the Golden State.

Fill a cocktail shaker with ice cubes. Add the vodka and St-Germain and shake well. Strain into a cracked-ice-filled double rocks glass. Stir in the grapefruit juice, then the ginger beer. Garnish with the twist.

Porch Crawler

"Lancelot" highball glass by Moser.

"CIRCO DI TIVOLI" WALLPAPER FROM STARK WALLCOVERING.

Salt Air Margarita

José Andrés · Minibar by José Andrés, Washington, DC

MARGARITA

Ice

1½ ounces blanco tequila

1 ounce Cointreau or other triple sec

1 ounce fresh lime juice

SALT AIR

4 ounces water

2 ounces fresh lime juice

1½ teaspoons salt

1½ teaspoons Sucro

Andrés uses Sucro, a powdered emulsifier beloved by avant-garde chefs, to make the salty foam topping. It's available at tienda.com.

1 MAKE THE MARGARITA Fill a cocktail shaker with ice. Add the tequila, Cointreau and lime juice and shake well. Strain into a chilled coupe.

2 MAKE THE SALT AIR Combine all of the ingredients in a large bowl. Using an immersion blender, mix until bubbles form. Carefully spoon on top of the drink.

Oishino

Wylie Dufresne · WD-50, Manhattan

Ice

2 ounces *junmai* sake

2 ounces coconut water

½ ounce cachaça

½ teaspoon Simple Syrup (p. 18)

"I often get inspired by ingredients that Wylie's using in the kitchen," says mixologist Tona Palomino about his collaborations with Dufresne. Recently, Dufresne used coconut water in a pork dish, and both men thought the lightly sweet liquid could work in a cocktail. They mixed it with earthy *junmai* sake, then added cachaça for bite.

Fill a pint glass with ice. Add all of the remaining ingredients and stir well. Strain into a chilled martini glass.

152

 # The Heirloom

Johnny Iuzzini · Jean Georges, Manhattan

- 7 Concord grapes or ¾ ounce Concord grape juice
- ½ ounce fresh lime juice

Ice

- 1½ ounces Old Tom gin
- ½ ounce Cynar
- ¼ ounce Strega (saffron-infused liqueur)
- 2 spritzes of diluted Aftelier anise hyssop essence or spearmint essence (optional)

On a night off from Jean Georges, pastry chef Iuzzini guest-bartended at the East Village bar PDT and created this cocktail. The sweet licorice–flavored anise hyssop essence he spritzes on the drink is frequently available at aftelier.com; spearmint essence always is.

In a cocktail shaker, muddle the grapes with the lime juice. Add ice and the gin, Cynar and Strega and shake well. Strain into a chilled coupe, then spritz the hyssop essence over the drink.

 # Tamarind Whiskey Sour

Andy Ricker · Pok Pok, Portland, OR

Ice

- 1½ ounces bourbon
- 1 ounce fresh lime juice
- 1 tablespoon tamarind paste mixed with 1 tablespoon hot water and cooled
- ½ ounce Rich Simple Syrup (p. 18)
- 1 orange slice and 1 jarred sour cherry (optional), for garnish

At his funky Thai restaurant, Ricker uses ingredients for his drinks that match the flavors of his food: sour, sweet, aromatic and even a little salty. This tamarind-spiked whiskey sour has been one of his best sellers since he created it four years ago.

Fill a cocktail shaker with ice. Add all of the remaining ingredients except the garnishes; shake well. Pour into a chilled double rocks glass and garnish with the orange and cherry. Serve with a wide straw.

153

Four on the Floor

David Lentz • The Hungry Cat, Los Angeles

Ice
- 1 ounce bourbon
- 1 ounce blended Scotch
- 1 ounce Carpano Antica Formula or other sweet vermouth
- 1 ounce maraschino liqueur
- 1 orange twist, for garnish

The name of mixologist Jeremy Allen's collaboration with Lentz refers to two things: the equal proportions of its four ingredients—bourbon, Scotch, vermouth and maraschino liqueur—and the love the men share for four-speed muscle cars.

Fill a pint glass with ice. Add all of the remaining ingredients except the garnish and stir well. Strain into a chilled coupe and garnish with the orange twist.

 ## DCV

Linton Hopkins • Restaurant Eugene, Atlanta

- 1 tablespoon sugar
- 1 teaspoon cinnamon
- 1 lime wedge
- Ice
- 1½ ounces Calvados
- 1 ounce Cointreau
- ¼ ounce St. Elizabeth Allspice Dram
- 1 ounce fresh lime juice
- ½ ounce fresh lemon juice
- ½ ounce Simple Syrup (p. 18)
- 1 apple slice, for garnish

Hopkins named this Calvados-based twist on a sidecar after the Citroën 2CV, known informally as a Deux Chevaux.

On a plate, mix the sugar and cinnamon. Moisten the outer rim of a martini glass or coupe with the lime wedge and coat lightly with the cinnamon sugar. Fill a cocktail shaker with ice. Add all of the remaining ingredients except the garnish and shake well. Strain into the prepared glass and garnish with the apple slice.

DCV

*"Mitos" Champagne coupe
by Květná from TableArt.*

CHEFS' COCKTAILS

The King

Tim Love · Love Shack, Fort Worth, TX

Ice

3 ounces Crown Royal Black Canadian whisky

1½ ounces blood orange liqueur

½ ounce Black Lime Syrup (below)

1 pitted cherry and 1 blood orange wheel, for garnish

Love, whose specialty is all things meat (burgers, steaks), says this variation on an old-fashioned is just the kind of cocktail he likes while sitting around the fire at his ranch after a day of hunting. He prefers making it with Crown Royal, "the unofficial whisky of Texas," he says. The black lime powder he uses in the syrup is sour and citrusy, with a subtle fermented flavor; sometimes called *omani,* it's available at kalustyans.com.

Fill a cocktail shaker with ice. Add all of the remaining ingredients except the garnish and shake well. Strain into an ice-filled double rocks glass and garnish with the cherry and blood orange wheel.

BLACK LIME SYRUP

Bring 4 ounces water to a boil and add ½ teaspoon black lime powder. Stir and simmer for 5 minutes, then add ½ cup sugar and stir until dissolved. Remove from the heat, cover and let stand for 10 minutes. Transfer to a jar and refrigerate for up to 1 week. Makes about 6 ounces.

The King

*"Frosted Paillette" double old-fashioned
glass by Kim Seybert from Barneys New York.*

MOCKTAILS

Honey & Spice, P. 167
"Aliseo" flute by NasonMoretti.

JENNIFER COLLIAU

Like most expert mocktail makers, Jennifer Colliau is an ingredient purist. Bartender at San Francisco's Slanted Door and owner of the artisanal syrup company Small Hand Foods, she uses real almonds (not extract) for the orgeat in her Almond-Fennel Cooler (p. 168) and makes grenadine from fresh pomegranate juice and unrefined cane sugar (no Red Dye no. 40 here). Colliau often looks to history for inspiration: "There are far more temperance drinks in old bar books than I had originally thought."

 ## Red Berry Shrub

Ice

2 tablespoons sour cherry preserves

8 raspberries, plus 3 raspberries skewered on a pick for garnish

½ ounce raspberry vinegar

½ ounce Simple Syrup (p. 18)

6 ounces chilled club soda

"Shrub" refers both to a syrup made from fruit, sugar and vinegar *and* to a drink made with said syrup. The vinegar, says Colliau, acts as "a lovely, unusual acidifier," replacing the citrus juice typically found in cocktails.

Fill a cocktail shaker with ice. Add all of the remaining ingredients except the club soda and garnish and shake well. Pour through a fine strainer into a chilled collins glass. Stir in the club soda and garnish with the skewered raspberries.

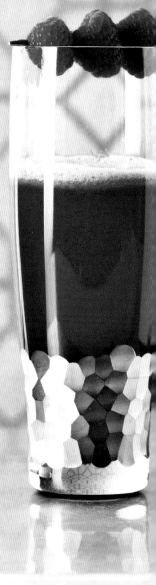

Red Berry Shrub

"Platinum Paillette" tumblers by Kim Seybert from Barneys New York.

"OCTAVIO" WALLPAPER BY MULBERRY FOR LEE JOFA.

MOCKTAILS

 ## Badminton Cooler

6 juniper berries
Five ½-inch-thick cucumber
    slices, plus 1 cucumber
    slice for garnish
Ice
20 mint leaves, plus 1 mint
    sprig for garnish
1 ounce fresh lime juice
1 ounce Simple Syrup
    (p. 18)
3 ounces chilled club
    soda

For this spin on a gin cocktail made with lime juice, cucumber and mint, Colliau uses juniper berries to approximate the flavor of the gin. The dried berries are available in the spice section of most supermarkets.

In a cocktail shaker, muddle the juniper with 5 cucumber slices. Add ice and the mint leaves, lime juice and Simple Syrup; shake well. Fine strain into an ice-filled collins glass. Stir in the soda and garnish with a cucumber slice and mint sprig.

 ## Rio Tropical

Ice
2 ounces coconut water
1 ounce fresh lime juice
¾ ounce pineapple gum
    syrup (thickened
    pineapple-flavored
    simple syrup)
¼ ounce orgeat (almond-
    flavored syrup)
1 mint sprig, smacked
    (p. 16), for garnish

San Francisco mixologist Jackie Patterson created this smooth, rich drink using Colliau's artisanal pineapple gum syrup and orgeat (both available at smallhandfoods. com). Patterson made a name for herself in the local bartending community by consistently winning cocktail competitions.

Fill a cocktail shaker with ice. Add all of the remaining ingredients except the garnish. Shake well and strain into an ice-filled collins glass. Garnish with the mint.

Antilles Tea

Ice
- 2 ounces chilled brewed lemongrass tea
- 1 ounce Clove Syrup (below)
- 1 ounce fresh lime juice
- 1 lime wheel studded with cloves, for garnish

"Tea," says Colliau, "is a wonderful base for nonalcoholic drinks because its slight bitterness makes a complex, adult beverage rather than a fruity kids' drink." Here she mixes lemongrass tea with an easy-to-make clove-infused simple syrup.

Fill a cocktail shaker with ice. Add the tea, Clove Syrup and lime juice and shake well. Strain into an ice-filled collins glass and garnish with the clove-studded lime wheel.

CLOVE SYRUP

In a spice grinder, coarsely grind 1½ teaspoons whole cloves. In a small saucepan, combine the ground cloves with 8 ounces water and bring to a boil. Remove from the heat, cover and let stand for 20 minutes. Pour through a fine strainer into a jar. Add 1 cup sugar, cover and shake gently until dissolved. Refrigerate for up to 1 month. Makes about 12 ounces.

MOCKTAILS

Juniper Tea Fizz

2 ounces chilled brewed green tea

1 ounce fresh lime juice

1 ounce Juniper Syrup (below)

1 large egg white

Ice

2 ounces chilled club soda

1 orchid or 1 lime wheel skewered with a juniper berry, for garnish

In cocktail lingo, a fizz is a drink that contains a spirit (often gin), citrus juices, sugar and club soda. The Silver Fizz is a gin fizz that includes an egg white, which adds foam and body to a shaken drink. In this Silver Fizz variation, Colliau uses juniper-infused syrup to hint at the flavor of gin.

In a cocktail shaker, combine the tea, lime juice, Juniper Syrup and egg white and shake well. Add ice and shake again. Pour through a fine strainer into a chilled fizz glass. Stir in the club soda; garnish with an orchid or a skewered lime wheel.

JUNIPER SYRUP

In a spice grinder, coarsely grind 1 tablespoon juniper berries. In a small saucepan, combine the ground juniper with 8 ounces water and bring to a boil. Remove from the heat, cover and let stand for 20 minutes. Pour through a fine strainer into a jar. Add 1 cup sugar, cover and shake gently until dissolved. Refrigerate for up to 1 month. Makes about 12 ounces.

Juniper Tea Fizz

*"18th Century–Inspired" water glass
by BollenGlass from John Derian.*

MOCKTAILS

Tropical Reunion

1 tablespoon pink
  peppercorns
Four 1-inch chunks of fresh
  pineapple
Ice
2 ounces chilled brewed
  green tea
½ ounce agave nectar
1 grapefruit twist, for
  garnish

Pink peppercorns have a tropical, warm, spicy quality that Colliau likes: "They really punch up fresh pineapple." To keep some of the crushed peppercorns in the drink, she often pours the tea mixture through a julep strainer (p. 12) instead of a fine strainer.

In a cocktail shaker, muddle the pink peppercorns. Add the pineapple; muddle again. Add ice, the tea and agave nectar; shake well. Fine strain into an ice-filled double rocks glass. Garnish with the twist.

Pear Balm

1 lemon twist
2 orange twists
½ juicy ripe pear, cored
Ice
3 ounces chilled strong-
  brewed green tea
¾ ounce elderflower
  syrup (available at
  farawayfoods.com)
¼ ounce fresh lemon juice

"I really enjoy off-dry aperitifs like cava, and this drink is in that vein," says Colliau. The ripe pear combined with lemon juice and green tea is refreshing and simple. "It stimulates the appetite without filling you up."

In a cocktail shaker, muddle the lemon twist with 1 orange twist. Add the pear and muddle again. Add ice and the tea, elderflower syrup and lemon juice; shake well. Fine strain into a chilled coupe and garnish with the remaining orange twist.

Honey & Spice

Ice
1½ ounces fresh grapefruit juice
1 ounce fresh lime juice
1 tablespoon honey mixed with 1 tablespoon warm water
½ ounce Allspice Syrup (below)
2 thin grapefruit twists, for garnish

When Colliau creates fruity drinks, she often adds at least one unexpected ingredient. Here, she pairs grapefruit and honey—which together have a terrific Creamsicle-like flavor—with allspice.

Fill a cocktail shaker with ice. Add all of the remaining ingredients except the garnish and shake well. Strain into an ice-filled collins glass and garnish with the grapefruit twists.

ALLSPICE SYRUP

In a spice grinder, coarsely grind 1 tablespoon allspice berries. In a small saucepan, combine the ground allspice with 8 ounces water and bring to a boil. Remove from the heat, cover and let stand for 20 minutes. Pour through a fine strainer into a jar. Add 1 cup sugar, cover and shake gently until dissolved. Refrigerate for up to 1 month. Makes about 12 ounces.

MOCKTAILS

 ## Almond-Fennel Cooler

¾ ounce orgeat (almond-
flavored syrup)

¾ ounce Fennel Syrup
(below)

½ ounce fresh lemon juice

Ice

6 ounces chilled club
soda

1 fennel frond, for
garnish (optional)

"Growing up in Northern California, I loved the smell of the wild fennel that grows along so many roads and waterways," Colliau says. That memory inspired this anise-accented drink, made with a fennel-infused simple syrup. For the orgeat, she advises using one made from almonds, not just extract. "True almond-based syrups add a satisfying richness."

In a collins glass, combine the orgeat, Fennel Syrup and lemon juice and stir well. Add ice, stir in the club soda and garnish with the fennel frond.

FENNEL SYRUP

In a spice grinder, coarsely grind 1 tablespoon fennel seeds. In a small saucepan, combine the ground seeds with 8 ounces water and bring to a boil. Remove from the heat, cover and let stand for 20 minutes. Pour through a fine strainer into a jar. Add 1 cup sugar, cover and shake gently until dissolved. Refrigerate for up to 1 month. Makes about 12 ounces.

168

Almond-Fennel Cooler

*"Herringbone" water glass
by Calvin Klein Home.*

Bitter Orange & Black Pepper Soda

Ice
- 2 tablespoons bitter orange marmalade
- 1 ounce fresh lemon juice
- ¾ ounce Black Pepper Syrup (below)
- 3 ounces chilled club soda
- ½ orange slice and a pinch of freshly ground pepper, for garnish

When Colliau travels to New York, she always makes time for a meal at Franny's, an artisanal pizza spot in Brooklyn that serves a great house-made sour orange soda. Because sour oranges can be difficult to find, Colliau opts for bitter orange marmalade in her version of the drink.

Fill a cocktail shaker with ice. Add the marmalade, lemon juice and Black Pepper Syrup and shake well. Pour through a fine strainer into an ice-filled double rocks glass. Stir in the club soda and garnish with the orange slice and ground pepper.

BLACK PEPPER SYRUP

In a spice grinder, coarsely grind 1 tablespoon black peppercorns. In a small saucepan, combine the ground pepper with 8 ounces water and bring to a boil. Remove from the heat, cover and let stand for 20 minutes. Pour through a fine strainer into a jar. Add 1 cup sugar, cover and shake gently until dissolved. Refrigerate for up to 1 month. Makes about 12 ounces.

MOCKTAILS

 ## Traverse Colada

Ice
1½ ounces cream of coconut from a well-shaken can
2½ tablespoons sour cherry preserves
½ ounce fresh lime juice
6 ounces chilled club soda
1 lime wheel, for garnish

During the years Colliau experimented with vegan cooking, she used ingredients like nuts and coconut instead of dairy products to add richness to food. For the Traverse Colada, she calls for cream of coconut, a thick, sweetened liquid made from fresh coconuts.

Fill a cocktail shaker with ice. Add the cream of coconut, cherry preserves and lime juice; shake well. Strain into an ice-filled collins glass, stir in the club soda and garnish with the lime wheel.

 ## Black Tea Sour

2 ounces chilled brewed black tea
¾ ounce fresh lemon juice
½ ounce grenadine, preferably homemade (p. 18)
1 large egg white
¼ ounce Simple Syrup (p. 18)
Ice

"Often it's difficult to construct nonalcoholic drinks without making them fruity sugar bombs," says Colliau. She admires this drink, created by cocktail purist Thad Vogler, because it's a straightforward sour that uses tea instead of a spirit as its base. (A huge tea fan, Vogler drinks several cups a day.)

In a cocktail shaker, combine all of the ingredients except ice and shake well. Add ice and shake again. Pour through a fine strainer into a chilled coupe.

"IMPERIAL TRELLIS" WALLPAPER BY SCHUMACHER.

PARTY FOOD

Lola Burgers, P. 201

PARTY FOOD

Numb Nuts

Sang Yoon · Lukshon, Culver City, CA

TOTAL: 15 MIN

MAKES ABOUT 3 CUPS

- 1 tablespoon Sichuan peppercorns
- 2 dried red chiles, stemmed
- 2 cups salted roasted Spanish peanuts
- 1 cup salted roasted cashews
- 1 tablespoon Asian fish sauce
- 1 teaspoon ground ginger
- 1 teaspoon onion powder
- 1 teaspoon garlic powder
- 2 teaspoons sugar
- 2 tablespoons vegetable oil
- 1 teaspoon Asian chile oil

The "numb" in the name of Yoon's recipe refers to the tongue-tingling Sichuan peppercorns in the salty, chile-fired spice mix.

In a spice grinder, finely grind the Sichuan peppercorns with the chiles. Transfer the spices to a medium bowl and add the peanuts, cashews, fish sauce, ginger, onion and garlic powder, sugar, vegetable oil and chile oil. Stir to combine, then transfer to a large skillet and cook over high heat, stirring constantly, until the nuts are toasted and fragrant, about 4 minutes. Spread the nuts on a baking sheet to cool before serving.

Pimento Cheese

Andrew Brochu · Kith & Kin, Chicago

TOTAL: 15 MIN

MAKES 1½ CUPS

- ½ pound extra-sharp yellow cheddar cheese, coarsely shredded
- ¼ cup diced jarred roasted red peppers
- 2 tablespoons minced shallots
- 2 tablespoons mayonnaise
- 1 tablespoon buttermilk or plain yogurt

Salt

Tabasco

Crackers, for serving

The largely Southern-born kitchen crew at Kith & Kin love this tangy, creamy Southern spread. It's great on crackers or sandwiched between slices of soft white bread for a delectable lunch.

In a medium bowl, combine the cheddar with the roasted peppers, shallots, mayonnaise and buttermilk. Season with salt and Tabasco. Transfer the mixture to a food processor and pulse 2 or 3 times, just until the cheese is finely chopped but not creamy. Transfer the Pimento Cheese to a bowl and serve with crackers.

PARTY FOOD

Fried Peppers with Prosciutto

Jenn Louis • Lincoln Restaurant, Portland, OR

TOTAL: 15 MIN

4 TO 6 SERVINGS

- 1 tablespoon olive oil
- 10 ounces Padrón or shishito peppers
- 5 thin slices of prosciutto (about 2 ounces), cut into ¼-inch-wide strips
- 1 tablespoon chopped mint

Fine sea salt

Spanish cooks traditionally fry sweet-hot Padrón peppers (available at melissas.com) and toss them with salt. Adding prosciutto and mint makes the peppers extraordinary.

In a large nonstick skillet, heat the olive oil. Add the peppers and cook over moderate heat, stirring often, until slightly charred and just softened, about 4 minutes. Add the prosciutto and cook until heated through, about 1 minute longer. Remove from the heat and toss with the mint. Season with salt, transfer to a plate and serve.

Fried Peppers with Prosciutto

"Inca" salad plate by Daniel Levy Porcelain;
gold table runner from ABC Carpet & Home.

Homemade Peanut Butter with a Side of Bacon

Eric Ottensmeyer • Leon's Full Service, Decatur, GA

TOTAL: 30 MIN

ABOUT 12 SERVINGS

- 1 **pound sliced bacon**
- 2 **cups unsalted roasted peanuts**
- ¼ **cup plus 2 tablespoons vegetable oil**
- 1 **tablespoon honey**

Salt

Peanut butter and bacon are a classic sandwich combination. Ottensmeyer serves them "chips and dip" style at Leon's.

————◇◈◇————

1 In a large nonstick skillet, cook the bacon in batches over moderate heat until crisp, about 10 minutes per batch. Transfer to paper towels to drain and let cool completely.
2 Meanwhile, in a food processor, blend the peanuts with the oil until very smooth. Add the honey, season with salt and pulse to combine. Serve with the bacon.

Ensaladilla Rusa Deviled Eggs

Haidar Karoum • Estadio, Washington, DC

TOTAL: 30 MIN

12 SERVINGS

- 1 medium Yukon Gold potato, peeled and cut into ½-inch pieces
- 1 small carrot, cut into ¼-inch dice
- 12 large hard-cooked eggs, peeled and halved lengthwise
- ¼ cup plus 2 tablespoons mayonnaise
- 1 tablespoon chopped parsley, plus more for garnish
- 1 teaspoon sherry vinegar

Salt

- 1 celery rib, finely diced
- 3 tablespoons minced white onion

One 6-ounce can oil-packed tuna, drained and flaked

While visiting tapas bars in San Sebastián, Spain, Karoum was inspired to create this riff on an American favorite, deviled eggs. He spikes these with the flavors of a traditional Spanish potato salad (*ensaladilla rusa*).

1 In a medium saucepan of boiling salted water, cook the potato and carrot over high heat until tender, about 5 minutes. Drain and let cool.

2 Carefully scoop the hard-cooked egg yolks into a large bowl and mash with a fork. Add the mayonnaise, the 1 tablespoon of parsley and the vinegar and season with salt. Fold in the potato, carrot, celery, onion and tuna. Mound the mixture in the egg halves and arrange on a platter. Garnish with parsley and serve.

PARTY FOOD

Spiced Crab Tacos

Michael Psilakis • FishTag, Manhattan

TOTAL: 25 MIN

4 SERVINGS

- 2 **medium tomatoes, finely chopped**
- 2 **large red radishes, cut into ¼-inch dice**
- ½ **small red onion, finely chopped**
- ¼ **cup chopped cilantro**
- 2 **teaspoons Sriracha chile sauce**

Salt

- 1 **large jalapeño**
- ½ **red bell pepper, cut into ⅓-inch dice**
- ½ **yellow bell pepper, cut into ⅓-inch dice**
- 3 **tablespoons extra-virgin olive oil**
- 1 **tablespoon fresh lime juice**
- 1 **tablespoon chopped mint**
- ½ **pound lump crabmeat, picked over for shell**

Eight 10-inch flour tortillas, halved or quartered

Psilakis's bright, fresh crab tacos incorporate traditional Latin ingredients and a hit of Asian chile sauce. Cooked shrimp would be great here as well.

⸻◇⸻

1 In a medium bowl, combine the tomatoes, radishes, red onion, 2 tablespoons of the cilantro and the Sriracha. Season the salsa with salt.
2 Light a grill or preheat a grill pan. Grill the jalapeño over moderate heat, turning, until charred all over. Let cool, then discard the charred skin, stem and seeds. Finely chop the jalapeño.
3 In another medium bowl, combine the jalapeño, red and yellow bell peppers, olive oil, lime juice, mint and the remaining 2 tablespoons of cilantro. Gently fold in the crabmeat and season with salt.
4 Grill the tortillas over high heat until puffed and charred in spots, about 20 seconds per side. Serve the spiced crab with the warm tortillas and salsa.

Spiced Crab Tacos

PARTY FOOD

Creamy Onion Dip

Vinny Dotolo & Jon Shook • Animal, Los Angeles

TOTAL: 1 HR

MAKES ABOUT 2 CUPS

- 1 tablespoon unsalted butter
- 2 yellow onions, thinly sliced (4 cups)
- 1½ cups sour cream
- 2 tablespoons snipped chives
- 2 teaspoons Worcestershire sauce
- 1 teaspoon garlic powder
- 1 teaspoon onion powder
- ½ teaspoon freshly ground pepper

Salt

Potato chips, carrot sticks and breadsticks, for serving

Shook and Dotolo's dip is a perfect update of the soup-mix-and-sour-cream classic: rich, savory and slightly sweet. After all, the chef-partners say, "What's better with a few cocktails than chips and a killer onion dip?"

In a deep, medium skillet, melt the butter. Add the onions, cover and cook over moderate heat, stirring occasionally, until softened, about 5 minutes. Uncover and cook, stirring frequently, until very tender and caramelized, about 30 minutes. Add a few tablespoons of water to the skillet as necessary to prevent scorching. Transfer the onions to a bowl and let cool. Stir in the sour cream, chives, Worcestershire, garlic powder, onion powder and pepper and season with salt. Serve with potato chips, carrots and breadsticks.

Carrot Bruschetta

Gerard Craft & Adam Altnether · Taste, St. Louis

TOTAL: 30 MIN

4 SERVINGS

Twelve ⅓-inch-thick baguette slices, cut on the diagonal

1 tablespoon extra-virgin olive oil, plus more for brushing

1 garlic clove

4 medium carrots, very thinly sliced, preferably on a mandoline

½ tablespoon unsalted butter

1 teaspoon fresh lemon juice

2 tablespoons chopped mint

Salt and freshly ground pepper

The short list of small plates complements the cocktails at Taste. These light bruschetta are terrific with In a Pickle (gin, St-Germain, Velvet Falernum, lime juice, dill and cucumber).

◇◇◇

1 Preheat the oven to 350°. Arrange the baguette slices on a baking sheet and brush on both sides with olive oil. Bake for about 10 minutes, until golden brown. Rub the hot toasts on one side with the garlic clove.

2 In a large skillet, heat the 1 tablespoon of olive oil. Add the carrots, cover and cook over moderate heat, tossing a few times, until golden brown and just tender, about 5 minutes. Remove from the heat and stir in the butter and lemon juice. Add the mint and season with salt and pepper. Top the toasts with the carrot mixture and serve.

PARTY FOOD

Fried Goat Cheese Balls with Honey

Victoria Moore • The Lazy Goat, Greenville, SC

TOTAL: 1 HR

8 SERVINGS

One 10-ounce log of fresh
    goat cheese
1 large egg, lightly
    beaten
1 cup club soda
¾ cup all-purpose flour
¼ cup cornstarch
Salt
3 cups *panko* (Japanese
    bread crumbs), lightly
    crushed
Canola oil, for frying
Honey, chopped roasted
    pistachios and freshly
    ground pepper, for
    serving

Club soda lightens the egg batter that coats the cheese, and a double-coating of *panko* crumbs amplifies the crunch. Moore serves the sweet-savory balls as an appetizer or a dessert.

1 Cut the goat cheese log into 16 pieces and roll each piece into a ball. Refrigerate the balls on a wax paper–lined baking sheet until firm, about 10 minutes.
2 In a bowl, whisk the egg and club soda. Gradually whisk in the flour and cornstarch and season with salt. Spread the *panko* in a shallow bowl. Dip the goat cheese balls in the egg batter, then dredge in the *panko*. Coat the balls again in egg batter and *panko*. Return them to the baking sheet and freeze just until firm, about 15 minutes.
3 In a large saucepan, heat 2 inches of canola oil to 375°. Working in batches, fry the cheese balls over high heat, turning occasionally, until golden and crisp, about 2 minutes. Using a slotted spoon, transfer the balls to a paper towel–lined plate and season with salt. Transfer the cheese balls to a platter, drizzle with honey and sprinkle with pistachios and pepper. Serve hot.

184

Fried Goat Cheese Balls with Honey

PARTY FOOD

Thrice-Cooked Fries

April Bloomfield · The Breslin, Manhattan

ACTIVE: 1 HR; TOTAL: 3 HR

4 SERVINGS

   4 large baking potatoes
      (¾ pound each),
      scrubbed but not
      peeled
Kosher salt
Vegetable oil, for frying

These fries have a cult following at The Breslin. Boiling makes the potatoes tender; double-frying makes them insanely crispy.

———◇◇◇———

1 Cut the potatoes into ⅓-inch-thick steak fries and transfer to a bowl of cold water. Bring a large pot of salted water to a boil. Drain the potatoes, add them to the pot and boil just until tender, about 5 minutes. Carefully drain the potatoes and transfer them to a paper towel–lined rack to cool. Refrigerate until chilled, about 1 hour.
2 In a large, deep skillet, heat 2 inches of oil to 250°. Set a rack over a baking sheet. Working in batches, fry the potatoes just until they begin to brown around the edges, about 8 minutes. Transfer the potatoes to the rack and let cool.
3 When all of the potatoes have been fried once, heat the oil to 350°. Fry the potatoes again, in batches, until golden and crisp, about 7 minutes per batch. Drain the fries on a paper towel–lined baking sheet, sprinkle with salt and serve.

Buffalo Fried Pickles

David Bull · Second Bar + Kitchen, Austin

TOTAL: 20 MIN

4 SERVINGS

Vegetable oil, for frying

2 kosher dill pickles (about 6 inches long), sliced lengthwise ¼ inch thick

All-purpose flour, for dredging

2 large eggs beaten with 2 tablespoons water

1 cup fine dry bread crumbs mixed with 1 teaspoon cayenne pepper

Blue cheese salad dressing and hot sauce, for serving

These salty, spicy pickles are one of Bull's favorite dishes at Second Bar + Kitchen, where they're served with a house-made Gorgonzola sauce. He likes pairing them with the bar's Fightin' Words cocktail, a corn-whiskey riff on a gin-based classic called the Last Word.

———————◇◇◇———————

1 In a large saucepan, heat 1½ inches of oil to 375°. Pat the pickle slices dry with paper towels. Put the flour, eggs and bread crumbs in 3 separate shallow bowls. Dredge the pickle slices in flour, shaking off the excess. Dip them in the egg, then coat with the bread crumbs. **2** Fry the pickles, about 5 slices at a time, turning once, until browned and crisp, about 1 minute. Transfer to paper towels to drain. Serve hot, with blue cheese dressing and hot sauce.

PARTY FOOD

Shrimp a la Plancha with Pimentón & Garlic Oil

Jalinson Rodriguez • Mercat, Manhattan

ACTIVE: 10 MIN; TOTAL: 1 HR
15 MIN

4 SERVINGS

- 3 garlic cloves, halved
- ½ cup plus 1 tablespoon extra-virgin olive oil
- 1 teaspoon pimentón de la Vera (smoked Spanish paprika)
- 12 large shrimp (about ½ pound), shelled and deveined
- Salt and freshly ground pepper
- Juice of ½ lemon
- 1 tablespoon chopped flat-leaf parsley
- Crusty bread, for serving

Shrimp with garlic is a traditional Spanish tapa; infusing the olive oil in the dish with garlic and smoked paprika, as here, adds lots of extra flavor. Make sure to have enough crusty bread on hand to soak up every last drop of oil.

❖❖❖

1 In a small saucepan, cook the garlic in ½ cup of the oil over very low heat for 30 minutes. Add the pimentón and cook for 30 minutes longer. Discard the garlic. Pour the oil into a heatproof bowl.
2 In a large nonstick skillet, heat the remaining 1 tablespoon of olive oil. Season the shrimp with salt and pepper, add them to the skillet and cook over moderate heat until opaque, about 1 minute per side. Remove the skillet from the heat and toss the shrimp with the lemon juice and parsley. Transfer the shrimp to a shallow bowl and drizzle with some of the garlic-pimentón oil. Serve the remaining oil alongside, with crusty bread.

**Shrimp a la Plancha
with Pimentón & Garlic Oil**

PARTY FOOD

Chickpea Fritters with Tapenade

Stephanie Izard · Girl & the Goat, Chicago

ACTIVE: 40 MIN; TOTAL: 1 HR
40 MIN

4 TO 6 SERVINGS

- 1 cup chickpea flour
- 2 cups water
- ½ cup freshly grated Parmigiano-Reggiano cheese
- ¼ cup canned chickpeas, chopped

Salt

- ½ cup pitted Niçoise olives, finely chopped
- ¼ preserved lemon, peel only, minced
- 1 tablespoon fresh lemon juice
- ½ teaspoon *sambal oelek* or other Asian chile paste
- ½ teaspoon honey
- 1 tablespoon chopped mint
- ¼ cup extra-virgin olive oil

Vegetable oil, for frying

Izard, the winner of *Top Chef* Season 4, eats cooked chickpeas straight from the can. Here, she turns them into crisp, Parmesan-spiked fritters served alongside a bold mix of olives, preserved lemon, mint, honey and chile paste.

——————◇◇◇——————

1 Line an 8-inch square baking pan with plastic wrap. In a medium saucepan, whisk the chickpea flour with the water until smooth. Cook over low heat, stirring constantly, until thick, about 5 minutes. Remove from the heat. Add the cheese and chickpeas, stir to combine and season with salt. Spread the mixture in the prepared pan in an even layer. Freeze until solid, about 1 hour.

2 Meanwhile, in a small bowl, combine the olives with the preserved lemon peel, lemon juice, *sambal,* honey, mint and olive oil. Set the tapenade aside.

3 Unmold the chickpea square, discard the plastic and cut into 1- to 1½-inch squares. In a large skillet, heat ½ inch of vegetable oil until shimmering. Cook the chickpea fritters in batches over high heat until golden and crisp, about 5 minutes. Drain the fritters on paper towels, sprinkle with salt and serve with the tapenade.

Fried Green Tomatoes with Shrimp Remoulade

Amy Tornquist • Watts Grocery, Durham, NC

TOTAL: 45 MIN

6 SERVINGS

- 6 ounces cooked medium shrimp, finely chopped
- 1 tablespoon chopped celery
- ⅓ cup mayonnaise
- 2 tablespoons snipped chives
- 1 tablespoon capers
- 1 tablespoon chopped flat-leaf parsley
- 1 teaspoon Dijon mustard
- 1 tablespoon fresh lemon juice
- 1½ teaspoons prepared horseradish

Salt and freshly ground black pepper

Cayenne pepper

- 4 green tomatoes, sliced crosswise ½ inch thick
- ¾ cup buttermilk
- ¾ cup all-purpose flour
- ¾ cup cornmeal

Vegetable oil, for frying

Tornquist serves both reinventions and tried-and-true versions of classic Southern dishes. These crunchy, tangy fried tomatoes with creamy, spicy shrimp remoulade are an unusual pairing of two low-country mainstays.

1 In a bowl, combine the shrimp with the celery, mayonnaise, chives, capers, parsley, mustard, lemon juice and horseradish. Season the remoulade with salt, black pepper and cayenne.
2 In a shallow bowl, coat the tomato slices with the buttermilk. In another shallow bowl, combine the flour and cornmeal and season with salt, black pepper and cayenne. Dip the tomato slices in the flour mixture, then transfer to a wax paper–lined baking sheet.
3 In a skillet, heat ½ inch of vegetable oil until shimmering. Add the tomatoes in batches and fry over high heat, turning once, until golden and crisp, about 5 minutes per batch. Drain on paper towels and season with salt and cayenne. Top with the shrimp remoulade and serve.

PARTY FOOD

East-Meets-West Wings

Nick Podesta & Jason Freiman • Duchamp, Chicago

ACTIVE: 35 MIN; TOTAL: 1 HR

4 SERVINGS

- 12 chicken wings
- 2 tablespoons vegetable oil
- Salt and freshly ground pepper
- ¾ cup rice vinegar
- ½ cup light brown sugar
- ¼ cup soy sauce
- 1½ tablespoons sweet Asian chile sauce
- 1½ teaspoons Sriracha chile sauce
- 2 tablespoons minced fresh ginger
- 2 scallions, sliced
- 1 tablespoon toasted sesame seeds

Podesta and Freiman put an Asian spin on chicken wings, the all-American bar snack, by coating them in a sweet-spicy-sticky glaze made with brown sugar, soy and chile sauces, chopped ginger and scallions.

1 Preheat the broiler. In a bowl, toss the chicken wings with the oil and season with salt and pepper. Arrange the wings on a rack set over a baking sheet and broil 10 to 12 inches from the heat for about 45 minutes, turning once or twice, until golden, crisp and cooked through.

2 Meanwhile, in a blender, combine the vinegar with the brown sugar, soy sauce, sweet chile sauce, Sriracha, ginger and half of the scallions and puree until very smooth. Transfer the sauce to a large saucepan and boil over high heat until thick and glossy, about 5 minutes. Add the chicken wings to the sauce and cook, tossing gently, until glazed, about 3 minutes. Transfer the wings to a platter and garnish with the remaining scallions and the sesame seeds.

East-Meets-West Wings

"Queen Anne" plate by dbO Home.

Cheese Fondue

Paulius Nasvytis · The Velvet Tango Room, Cleveland

TOTAL: 25 MIN

6 TO 8 SERVINGS

- ½ pound Gruyère cheese, cubed
- ½ pound Emmental cheese, cubed
- 3 tablespoons all-purpose flour
- 1¾ cups dry white wine
- 2 teaspoons kirsch
- ¼ teaspoon freshly grated nutmeg

Pinch of cayenne pepper

Salt

Crusty bread, for serving

This classic fondue has been a staple at the Velvet Tango Room for years. Owner Paulius Nasvytis encourages patrons who order it to follow traditional fondue etiquette: "If a man's chunk of crusty French bread falls into the pot, he has to buy the next round of drinks. If a woman's piece falls in, she has to kiss the man to her left."

In a medium bowl, toss the cheeses with the flour. In a medium saucepan, bring the wine to a simmer. Add the cheese mixture and cook over moderately low heat, stirring with a wooden spoon, until the cheese is melted and smooth, about 5 minutes. Stir in the kirsch, nutmeg and cayenne and season with salt. Serve hot, with crusty bread.

Stuffed Korean Fire Chiles

Craig Koketsu · The Hurricane Club, Manhattan

TOTAL: 45 MIN

6 SERVINGS

- 1 **pound ground pork**
- 2 **garlic cloves, minced**
- 1½ **tablespoons minced fresh ginger**
- 2 **scallions, minced**
- 2 **tablespoons oyster sauce**
- 1 **tablespoon toasted sesame oil**
- ½ **teaspoon sugar**

Salt and freshly ground pepper

Ten 6-inch Korean chiles or other medium-spicy chiles, halved lengthwise and seeded

- ½ **cup** *panko* **(Japanese bread crumbs)**

The Hurricane Club offers these savory stuffed chiles as part of its pupu platter, but using larger peppers, like Anaheims, turns the dish into a satisfying and impressive main course.

1 Preheat the oven to 425°. In a medium bowl, combine the pork with the garlic, ginger, scallions, oyster sauce, sesame oil, sugar and ½ teaspoon each of salt and pepper. Stuff the chiles with the pork mixture, pressing down on the stuffing.
2 Arrange the stuffed chiles filling side up on a baking sheet and sprinkle with the *panko*. Bake for about 15 minutes, until the chiles are tender and the meat is firm and no longer pink.
3 Preheat the broiler. Broil the stuffed chiles 8 to 10 inches from the heat for about 2 minutes, until the bread crumbs are golden. Transfer to a platter and serve.

Hello Kitty Hot Dogs

Daniel Wright • Senate, Cincinnati

TOTAL: 30 MIN

6 SERVINGS

- 1½ tablespoons wasabi powder
- 1 tablespoon water
- ¼ cup plus 2 tablespoons mayonnaise
- 1½ teaspoons sugar
- 8 cups shredded cabbage, preferably a mixture of green and red
- 1 small carrot, shredded
- 1½ tablespoons *ponzu* (Japanese citrus-soy sauce)

Salt

- 6 all-beef hot dogs
- 6 brioche hot dog buns, split
- 1 teaspoon black sesame seeds

Wright tops these inspired hot dogs with wasabi mayo and a *ponzu*-spiked cabbage and carrot slaw. Cutting a cross pattern into the ends of the dogs helps them get crispy.

1 In a medium bowl, whisk the wasabi powder with the water, then whisk in the mayonnaise and sugar.

2 In a large bowl, toss together the cabbage, carrot and *ponzu*. Add ¼ cup of the wasabi mayo and toss to coat. Season the slaw with salt.

3 Light a grill or preheat a grill pan. Cut a cross pattern into the ends of each hot dog. Grill over moderately high heat until lightly charred all over, about 4 minutes. Place a hot dog in each bun and top each with 1 teaspoon of the remaining wasabi mayonnaise. Spoon about 1 cup of slaw onto each hot dog, sprinkle with the sesame seeds and serve.

Hello Kitty Hot Dog

"Gold-brushed" ceramic sauce bowl from Ochre.

PARTY FOOD

Sautéed Calamari

Aaron Hinchy · Zig Zag Café, Seattle

ACTIVE: 25 MIN; TOTAL: 1 HR

4 TO 6 SERVINGS

- 1 head of garlic, halved crosswise
- ¼ cup extra-virgin olive oil, plus more for drizzling
- 2 teaspoons minced preserved lemon peel
- Pinch of dried oregano
- Salt and freshly ground pepper
- 2 teaspoons vegetable oil
- 1 pound cleaned small squid—patted dry, bodies cut into ¼-inch rings, large tentacles halved
- ¼ cup dry white wine
- 1 large plum tomato, chopped
- 1 tablespoon chopped pitted kalamata olives
- 1 tablespoon chopped drained capers
- ¼ teaspoon crushed red pepper
- 2 tablespoons chopped flat-leaf parsley
- Crusty bread, for serving

The chefs at Zig Zag hit on the fantastic sauce for this calamari while trying to use up some leftover preserved lemons. They now have to make gallons of preserved lemons every month to keep up with demand.

1 Preheat the oven to 350°. Set the garlic cut side up on a piece of foil and drizzle with olive oil. Wrap loosely in the foil and bake for about 40 minutes, until the garlic is very soft. Squeeze the garlic into a mini food processor. Add the preserved lemon, oregano and the ¼ cup of olive oil and process to a paste. Season the garlic paste with salt and pepper.

2 In a large skillet, heat the vegetable oil until shimmering. Add the squid and cook over high heat, tossing, until starting to turn opaque, about 1 minute. Season with salt and pepper and add the wine. Cook, stirring, until the wine has reduced by half, about 30 seconds. Stir in the tomato, olives, capers and crushed red pepper, then stir in the garlic paste and bring just to a simmer. Season with salt and pepper, top with the parsley and serve with crusty bread.

Duck & Sweet Potato Hash

Cure, New Orleans

ACTIVE: 35 MIN; TOTAL: 1 HR

6 SERVINGS

- 2 tablespoons vegetable oil
- 2 ounces serrano ham, finely diced
- 1 red onion, finely chopped
- 2 pounds sweet potatoes, peeled and cut into ½-inch pieces
- ½ teaspoon dried thyme

Salt and freshly ground pepper
- ½ cup dry vermouth
- 4 duck confit legs, skin and fat discarded, meat cut into ½-inch pieces
- 2 scallions, thinly sliced
- 6 large eggs

Hot sauce, for serving

According to Cure's former chef Jason McCullar, Louisianans eat more duck per capita than residents of any other state. So it seemed natural to him to combine it with sweet potatoes, another Southern staple. Served with fried eggs and hot sauce, the hash makes a terrific brunch dish or first course.

1 Preheat the oven to 350°. In a large ovenproof skillet, heat 1 tablespoon of the oil. Add the ham and cook over moderately high heat, stirring, until lightly browned, about 2 minutes. Add the onion and cook for 1 minute. Add the sweet potatoes and thyme, season with salt and pepper and cook just until the sweet potatoes are lightly browned in spots, 2 to 3 minutes. Add the vermouth and cook, scraping up any browned bits. Roast the hash in the oven for about 20 minutes, until the potatoes are tender. Stir in the duck and scallions and roast until heated through, about 5 minutes; keep warm.
2 Heat the remaining 1 tablespoon of oil in a large skillet. Working in 2 batches, fry the eggs over-easy over moderate heat, about 3 minutes. Transfer the hash to shallow bowls, top with the fried eggs and serve with hot sauce.

Mussels with Buttery Miso Broth

Tony Maws • Craigie on Main, Cambridge, MA

TOTAL: 30 MIN

4 SERVINGS

- 2 tablespoons unsalted butter, softened
- 2 tablespoons yellow miso paste
- ¼ cup extra-virgin olive oil
- 4 garlic cloves, thinly sliced
- ½ teaspoon crushed red pepper
- Pinch of saffron threads, crumbled
- 2 pounds mussels, scrubbed and debearded
- 2 tablespoons sake
- 1 tablespoon pastis or Pernod
- ¼ cup water
- 1 tablespoon chopped tarragon
- 1 tablespoon chopped parsley
- Crusty bread, for serving

Like the rest of Maws's dishes, these mussels can't be defined by a single style of cuisine. Seemingly disparate French, Spanish and Japanese flavors blend in this ingenious take on a French bar-food classic.

In a small bowl, blend the butter with the miso. In a large pot, heat the olive oil. Add the garlic and cook over moderately high heat until golden, about 1 minute. Using a slotted spoon, transfer the garlic to a plate. Add the crushed red pepper and saffron to the pot. Add the mussels and cook, stirring, until the shells begin to open, about 2 minutes. Stir in the sake and pastis. Add the water and miso butter and cook, stirring, until the mussels have opened and are coated with sauce. Discard any mussels that don't open. Stir in the herbs and garlic and serve in bowls with crusty bread.

Lola Burgers

Michael Symon • B Spot, Woodmere, OH

TOTAL: 35 MIN

4 SERVINGS

- 8 thick-cut slices of smoky bacon (½ pound)
- 1½ pounds mixed ground sirloin and chuck
- Kosher salt and freshly ground pepper
- 4 slices of smoked cheddar cheese (2 ounces)
- 4 large eggs
- 4 English muffins, toasted
- ¼ cup pickled cocktail onions, thinly sliced
- Ketchup and mustard, for serving

This iteration of Symon's crazy-delicious Lola burger—part hamburger, part breakfast sandwich—was adapted from his latest cookbook, *Michael Symon's Live to Cook.*

1 In a large nonstick skillet, cook the bacon over moderate heat until crisp, about 6 minutes. Drain on paper towels. Pour off all but 1 tablespoon of the bacon fat in the skillet.

2 Preheat a grill pan. Shape the meat into four 5-inch patties and season generously with salt and pepper. Grill over moderately high heat until lightly charred, about 3 minutes. Flip the burgers and top with the smoked cheddar. Cook for about 3 minutes longer for medium-rare meat.

3 Meanwhile, in the reserved bacon fat in the skillet, fry the eggs over-easy over moderate heat, about 3 minutes. Set the burgers on the bottoms of the English muffins and top with the pickled onions, bacon and fried eggs. Serve with ketchup and mustard.

Shepherd's Pie

Brian Hill • Shepherd's Pie, Rockport, ME

ACTIVE: 1 HR; TOTAL: 3 HR

6 SERVINGS

- 2 tablespoons extra-virgin olive oil
- 2 pounds trimmed lamb shoulder, cut into 1-inch pieces

Salt and freshly ground pepper

- 1 large carrot, cut into ¾-inch pieces
- 1 large onion, coarsely chopped
- 10 peeled garlic cloves
- 2 anchovy fillets
- 1 tablespoon drained capers
- 1 pound plum tomatoes, diced
- 1½ cups rainwater Madeira
- 1½ cups chicken stock or low-sodium broth
- 2½ pounds baking potatoes, peeled and cut into 2-inch chunks
- 1 stick unsalted butter, softened
- ¾ cup buttermilk

Rainwater Madeira, a fortified wine, gives Hill's pub dish a caramelly sweetness.

1 Preheat the oven to 325°. Heat the oil in an enameled cast-iron casserole. Season the lamb with salt and pepper; cook over high heat until browned all over, 15 minutes. Transfer to a plate. Add the carrot, onion, garlic, anchovies, capers and tomatoes to the casserole. Cook over moderate heat, stirring, until lightly browned, 8 minutes. Add the Madeira and bring to a boil; add the stock and bring to a boil. Return the lamb to the casserole; season with salt and pepper. Cover and braise in the oven for 1 hour, until tender.

2 Cook the potatoes in boiling salted water until tender, 20 minutes. Drain and cook the potatoes in the pot to evaporate any water. Add the butter and buttermilk and mash. Season with salt and pepper.

3 Raise the oven heat to 425°. Set the casserole over high heat and boil until the juices reduce by half, about 15 minutes. Mash the garlic into the juices. Spoon the stew into six 1½-cup ramekins; set on a sturdy baking sheet. Mound the potatoes on top; bake for 25 minutes, until browned in spots. Let rest 20 minutes, then serve.

Shepherd's Pie

"Hemisphere" plates in gold stripe (below) and Toundra Fall (below left) by J.L. Coquet from DeVine Corporation.

TOP 100 AMERICAN BARS

A listing of the country's best bars, lounges and restaurants, many of them contributors to this book.

EAST COAST

BOSTON

Drink Star chef Barbara Lynch's bar dispenses with menus; mixologist John Gertsen and his team custom-make drinks like the Golden State (p. 150) for each guest. *348 Congress St.; 617-695-1806; drinkfortpoint.com.*

Eastern Standard

Jackson Cannon, who contributed the Brandy chapter (p. 104), presides over Eastern Standard's 46-foot-long marble-topped bar at the luxe Hotel Commonwealth. *528 Commonwealth Ave.; 617-532-9100; eastern standardboston.com.*

Island Creek Oyster Bar

This bright, airy place serves all manner of surf and turf (including adorable fried-oyster sliders) alongside drinks like bar manager Bob McCoy's Puritan's Punch (p. 147). *500 Commonwealth Ave.; 617-532-5300; island creekoysterbar.com.*

NEW YORK CITY

Clover Club Named after a pre-Prohibition men's club, this stylish classic-cocktails spot is co-owned by Julie Reiner of Manhattan's renowned Flatiron Lounge. *210 Smith St., Brooklyn; 718-855-7939; cloverclubny.com.*

Death & Co.

Joaquín Simó and the other bartenders at this East Village destination have an encyclopedic knowledge of cocktails. Offerings include Simó's sherry-based Flor de Jerez (p. 138). *433 E. Sixth St., Manhattan; 212-388-0882; death andcompany.com.*

Dram A rotating team of star bartenders work the bar at Dram, offering oddities like barrel-aged Martinezes (with toasty charred-wood flavors) and cocktails on draft (an Aperol spritzer). *177 S. Fourth St., Brooklyn; 718-486-3726; drambar.com.*

Dutch Kills Modeled after an 1890s saloon, this bar co-owned by Richard Boccato (creator of the Rum chapter, p. 76) serves classic cocktails made with hand-cut ice. Live jazz and ragtime bands play throughout the week. *27-24 Jackson Ave., Long Island City; 718-383-2724; dutchkillsbar.com.*

Eleven Madison Park

Top-notch service is the hallmark of this elegant restaurant and bar. Head bartender Leo Robitschek serves up inventive drinks like the Mott & Mulberry (rye, Luxardo Amaro Abano, apple cider and lemon) to pair with chef Daniel Humm's divine cooking. *11 Madison Ave., Manhattan; 212-889-0905; elevenmadisonpark.com.*

Employees Only

This bartender-owned supper club was originally intended to be a late-night gathering spot for fellow bar and restaurant workers. *510 Hudson St., Manhattan; 212-242-3021; employeesonlynyc.com.*

Fort Defiance

Owned by St. John Frizell (formerly of Pegu Club), this café and bar opens at 8 a.m. for coffee and breakfast. By 9 on brunch days the bar opens, pouring house-carbonated sodas and stellar cocktails like the Warwick Bramble (blackberries, lemon and local black currant liqueur). *365 Van Brunt St., Brooklyn; 347-453-6672; fortdefiancebrooklyn.com.*

Lani Kai Classic-cocktail expert Julie Reiner opened this 1950s-style Hawaii-inspired spot in 2010. Tropical cocktails like her Isle of Islay Swizzle (p. 144) are served alongside tasty dishes such as the chile-and-sesame-spiked Tuna Poke. *525 Broome St., Manhattan; 646-596-8778; lanikainy.com.*

Little Branch At this subterranean lounge owned by Milk & Honey's Sasha Petraske and cocktail expert Joseph Schwartz, the sharply dressed staff mixes drinks with ice custom-made for each glass. *22 Seventh Ave. South, Manhattan; 212-929-4360; littlebranch.net.*

Mayahuel Death & Co. alum Philip Ward (creator of the Tequila chapter, p. 60) opened this East Village Mexican spot in 2009 with food by Luis and Vincent Gonzales and a cocktail menu dedicated to tequila and mezcal. *304 E. Sixth St., Manhattan; 212-253-5888; mayahuelny.com.*

Milk & Honey Bartenders in sleeve garters custom-make drinks at this tiny, reservations-only lounge with an unmarked entrance. *134 Eldridge St., Manhattan; mlkhny.com.*

Painkiller This new Polynesian-themed bar has been lauded for its well-researched and thoughtfully executed scorpion bowls, daiquiris and other kitschily presented tiki cocktails. *49 Essex St., Manhattan; 212-777-8454; painkillernyc.com.*

PDT Mixologist Jim Meehan, deputy editor of *Food & Wine Cocktails,* obsesses over obscure classic drinks at this excellent reservations-only lounge, whose name means Please Don't Tell. The (unmarked) door is in a phone booth inside the hot dog joint Crif Dogs. *113 Saint Marks Pl., Manhattan; 212-614-0386; pdtnyc.com.*

Pegu Club Audrey Saunders, a leader of the vintage cocktail movement, co-owns this mixologists' hangout, which serves its drinks with dropper bottles of fresh juices, bitters and simple syrup. *77 W. Houston St., Manhattan; 212-473-7348; peguclub.com.*

The Summit Bar The drink menu at Greg Seider's Alphabet City bar is divided into "Classic" and "Alchemist." The Situation (from the Alchemist section) mixes Afghani raisin–infused rye with caraway-infused agave, lemon juice and orange bitters. *133 Avenue C, Manhattan; no phone; thesummitbar.net.*

Vandaag Mixologist Katie Stipe focuses on aquavit and genever, both neat and in cocktails, at this airy new Northern European restaurant. Concoctions such as the B-Side Sling (genever, rooibos-infused vermouth, lemon juice and maraschino liqueur) are served alongside snacks like *bitterballen,* slow-braised oxtail croquettes. *103 Second Ave., Manhattan; 212-253-0470; vandaagnyc.com.*

Weather Up Tribeca The signature dim lighting and Paris Métro vibe of Weather Up's Brooklyn location also define Kathryn Weatherup's newly opened Tribeca space. Richard Boccato, who contributed the Rum chapter (p. 76), designed the stellar drink list. *159 Duane St., Manhattan; 212-766-3202.*

The Franklin Mortgage & Investment Co. Hidden in a building that fronted the largest alcohol-smuggling ring in the U.S. during Prohibition, this lounge maintains a speakeasy feel. Dapper bartenders serve spot-on classics, plus tasty new inventions like the Peckinpah (mezcal, rum, lime juice and blackberry-habanero syrup). *112 S. 18th St.; 267-467-3277; thefranklinbar.com.*

Noble Handlebar-mustachioed Christian Gaal makes his own tonic water and serves reinvented old-school drinks at this locavore's paradise. (There's a vegetable garden on the roof.) Don't miss chef Brinn Sinnott's house-made chorizo. *2025 Sansom St.; 215-568-7000; noblecookery.com.*

Southwark A pioneer in the resurgence of classic cocktails in Philadelphia, this corner restaurant and bar specializes in old-time drinks like Sazeracs, Jupiters and Mary Pickfords. They also have an impressive selection of ryes and gins. *701 S. Fourth St.; 215-238-1888; southwarkrestaurant.com.*

WASHINGTON, DC AREA

The Gibson This exclusive bar with a no-standing policy is all about well-crafted cocktails, both classic and innovative. The waitstaff flames twists over drinks tableside. *2009 14th St. NW, Washington, DC; 202-232-2156; thegibsondc.com.*

The Passenger Veteran bartenders and brothers Derek and Tom Brown run this menuless drink destination. It's divided into two distinct spaces: a raucous saloon with a punk-rock sound track (Tom's realm) and a quiet cocktail club (Derek's). *1021 Seventh St. NW, Washington, DC; 202-393-0220; passengerdc.com.*

PS 7's Known here for her Old Faithful Punch (p. 143), mixologist Gina Chersevani also whips up terrific martinis (with pickled wax beans) and other seasonal cocktails, like Seckel pear "Jelly Jars": rye, honey, vanilla, cinnamon and pears, served in 4-ounce jars. *777 I St. NW, Washington, DC; 202-742-8550; ps7restaurant.com.*

PX Todd Thrasher makes the cocktails at this chandelier-lit speakeasy (there's no sign outside, just a blue light). It's owned by the team behind the terrific Restaurant Eve. *728 King St., Alexandria, VA; 703-299-8384; restauranteve.com.*

GREAT LAKES/MIDWEST

CLEVELAND

The Velvet Tango Room A piano player accompanies the clinking of perfectly square ice cubes at this swank, living room–like cocktail purists' hangout. A short list of snacks includes a terrific Cheese Fondue (p. 194). *2095 Columbus Rd.; 216-241-8869; velvettangoroom.com.*

CHICAGO

Bar DeVille Owners Matt Eisler and Kevin Heisner describe the look of their neighborhood spot as "Parisian dive bar" (flea market furniture, vintage pool table, neon signage). Mixologist Brad Bolt serve excellent Sazeracs, swizzles and pisco sours as well as cans of PBR and Miller High Life. *701 N. Damen Ave.; 312-929-2349; bardeville.com.*

Double A Tad Carducci co-created the menu at this lounge below the restaurant Mercadito. With a focus on bottle service, Double A offers more than 25 tequila options, and guests can "interact" with bartenders at a "mixologist's table" while their drinks are being made. *108 W. Kinzie St.; doubleachicago.com.*

The Drawing Room

At this subterranean restaurant and lounge, visitors can have their drinks prepared from a custom-made bar cart, accompanied by a cocktail history lesson. *937 N. Rush St.; 312-266-2694; thedrchicago.com.*

Sable Kitchen & Bar

Master mixologist Jacques Bezuidenhout co-created the drink list for this elegant gastro-lounge. Behind the 40-foot bar, head bartender Mike Ryan serves his own creations, too, like the rhubarb-infused Bridal Shower (p. 140). *505 N. State St.; 312-755-9704; sablechicago.com.*

The Violet Hour

With chandeliers and a fireplace, this lounge is modeled after early-19th-century English clubs and French salons. Floor-to-ceiling curtains define three rooms, where guests enjoy concoctions like Baron's Brew (tea-infused gin, lemon juice, neroli-violet syrup and house-made tonic). *1520 N. Damen Ave.; 773-252-1500; theviolethour.com.*

The Whistler

While guests take in live music, film screenings, poetry readings and an art gallery, Paul McGee makes drinks like the Mamie Taylor: Scotch, ginger liqueur, ginger beer, lime and rosemary. *2421 N. Milwaukee Ave.; 773-227-3530; whistlerchicago.com.*

Bryant's Cocktail Lounge

Although Bryant's has been around since 1938, the two-story lounge looks as if time stopped there in 1976. There's no drink menu; customers are invited to order by spirit, flavor, strength, texture, size or even color. *1579 S. Ninth St.; 414-383-2620; bryants cocktaillounge.com.*

Distil More than 120 bourbons and ryes, along with local cheeses and charcuterie, are the draw at Distil. A recent "Taste of the Month" featured a bourbon old-fashioned infused with Wisconsin's famous Nueske's bacon. *722 N. Milwaukee St.; 414-220-9411; distilmilwaukee.com.*

Maduro Smoking of cigars and pipes (but not cigarettes) is welcome here. Maduro has a rotating selection of stogies and cocktails like the Ipanema (Licor 43, cachaça and orange and lime juices). *117 E. Main St.; 608-294-9371; madurocigarbar.com.*

Natt Spil This always busy restaurant is known for DJ-spun music and original concoctions. One to try: the Creole Napoleon, with rum, muddled ginger and spicy orange Créole Shrubb. *211 King St.; 608-258-8787; nattspil.com.*

Nostrano At Elizabeth and Timothy Dahl's terrific new Italian-inspired restaurant, mixologist Chad Vogel turns out barrel-aged Manhattans and inventions like Variable High Cloudiness & Gusty Winds, a Cynar-spiked take on a Dark & Stormy. *111 S. Hamilton St.; 608-395-3295; nostranomadison.com.*

MINNEAPOLIS
Bradstreet Craftshouse This restaurant has a drink menu by Toby Maloney (creator of the Flaming Heart on p. 144) and a private "parlour room" hidden behind a velvet curtain. *601 First Ave. N.; 612-312-1821; bradstreet craftshouse.com.*

ST. LOUIS
Taste Local hero Ted Kilgore mans the bar at this newly relocated small-plates spot, where Adam Altnether offers house-made pickles, deviled eggs and the

Carrot Bruschetta on p. 183. *4584 Laclede Ave.; 314-361-1200; tastebarstl.com.*

SOUTH

NASHVILLE
The Patterson House Toby Maloney designed the drink menu at this bar named for the Tennessee governor who vetoed the return of statewide Prohibition in 1909. *1711 Division St.; 615-636-7724; thepatterson nashville.com.*

DECATUR, GA
Leon's Full Service Not only does this restaurant in a former filling station make its own liqueurs and cocktail syrups, it has bar snacks worth traveling for, like Homemade Peanut Butter with a Side of Bacon (p. 178). *131 E. Ponce de Leon Ave.; 404-687-0500; leonsfullservice.com.*

ATLANTA
Holeman & Finch Public House From the team behind Restaurant Eugene, this gastropub serves Southern-inspired cocktails such as the Spice Bandit (p. 142) by mixologist Greg Best. *2277 Peachtree Rd.; 404-948-1175; holeman-finch.com.*

The Sound Table This restaurant organizes its drink list into categories like "Bright & Dry" (a grapefruity Paloma) and "Strong, Rich & Strange" (the Matterhorn: Old Tom gin, bianco vermouth, Chartreuse and pine liqueur in an absinthe-rinsed glass). It transforms into a dance club most nights around 11 p.m. *483 Edgewood Ave. SW; 404-835-2534; thesoundtable.com.*

MIAMI BEACH

The Florida Room The center of Miami Beach nightlife, Lenny Kravitz's updated 1950s Havana–style piano bar in the Delano has music played on a Lucite grand piano and Latin-inspired drinks from mixologist John Lermayer. *1685 Collins Ave.; 305-672-2000; delano-hotel.com.*

Living Room Leading Miami's craft-cocktail movement, the alchemists at this luxe lounge in the W Hotel use unusual ingredients like Sriracha (Thai hot sauce), roast herbs for cocktails with blowtorches and top drinks with flavored foams. *2201 Collins Ave.; 305-938-3000; wsouthbeach.com.*

NEW ORLEANS

Arnaud's French 75 Bar Chris Hannah (creator of the Contessa, p. 135) mans the bar at this dapper, cigar-friendly spot inside Arnaud's, one of New Orleans's oldest and most venerated restaurants. *813 Bienville St.; 504-523-5433; arnaudsrestaurant.com.*

Bar UnCommon Fourth-generation bartender Chris McMillian creates classic-inspired cocktails like ginger-spiked Manhattans at this stylish spot in the Pere Marquette hotel. *817 Common St.; 504-525-1111; baruncommon.com.*

Cure Bartenders at Cure use droppers to add house-made tinctures to their cocktails, which are served alongside tasty dishes like the Duck & Sweet Potato Hash on p. 199. *4905 Freret St.; 504-302-2357; curenola.com.*

HOUSTON

Anvil Bar & Refuge Two devotees of old-school cocktails serve flips, brambles, bucks and sours and host monthly themed cocktail classes at this bar in an old Bridgestone-Firestone tire shop. *1424 Westheimer Rd.; 713-523-1622; anvilhouston.com.*

AUSTIN

Haddingtons At this British-influenced tavern (think Scotch eggs and fish-and-chips), mixologist Bill Norris creates clever drinks like the Waldorf No. 2: apple brandy, nocino (walnut liqueur) and celery bitters. *601 W. Sixth St.; 512-992-0204; thehaddington.com.*

Péché In addition to terrific pre-Prohibition cocktails, Péché has nearly a dozen absinthes, including a beet-based one from France. *208 W. Fourth St.; 512-494-4011; pecheaustin.com.*

DALLAS/FORT WORTH

Bolsa On Wednesday nights at this airy industrial restaurant, bartenders make drinks using ingredients that guests have suggested via Facebook. A recent request for hard lemon candy resulted in the Hard Candy Cable Car: rum, orange liqueur and limoncello infused with the candy. *614 W. Davis St., Dallas; 214-367-9367; bolsadallas.com.*

The Usual Owner Brad Hensarling makes Sazeracs and other Prohibition-era cocktails at this gorgeously spare, modern bar. An unexpected feature: It's nonsmoking. *1408 W. Magnolia Ave., Fort Worth; 817-810-0114; theusualbar.com.*

Victor Tango's This small-plates and classic-cocktails spot is known for its fried chicken and waffles topped with pancetta gravy and maple syrup. *3001 N. Henderson Ave., Dallas; 214-252-8595; victortangos.com.*

SOUTHWEST

DENVER, BOULDER & ASPEN

The Bitter Bar Located in the Asian-inspired bistro Happy Noodle House, the Bitter Bar opens each night around 11, when the restaurant closes. Bar manager Mark Stoddard and his crew make some of Boulder's best pre-Prohibition cocktails. *835 Walnut St., Boulder; 303-442-3050; happy noodlehouse.com.*

Jimmy's Surrounded by the Rocky Mountains, this Aspen institution has more than 100 tequilas and mezcals, makes terrific margaritas and hosts legendary Saturday night Latin-dance parties. *205 S. Mill St., Aspen; 970-925-6020; jimmysaspen.com.*

Oak at Fourteenth Frasca Food & Wine alums Bryan Dayton and Steven Redzikowski co-own this newcomer,

where Dayton offers NA (nonalcoholic), LA (low-alcohol) and HA (high-alcohol) drinks; his Ginger's Lost Island (p. 146) is on the HA list. *1400 Pearl St., Boulder; 303-444-3622; oakatfourteenth.com.*

Steuben's A reimagined version of the classic American chrome-and-comfort-food diner, Steuben's serves bacon-infused-vodka Bloody Marys as well as Monte Cristos and fries. *523 E. 17th Ave., Denver; 303-830-1001; steubens.com.*

LAS VEGAS

Downtown Cocktail Room This spacious and subdued lounge in a renovated wedding chapel is marked by a tiny sign; inside are cool drinks like the Cat's Pajamas: gin, Campari, orange juice, Chartreuse and maple syrup. *111 Las Vegas Blvd. S.; 702-880-3696; thedowntownlv.com.*

Herbs & Rye Although this restaurant is designed to resemble a kitschy 1960s Italian place, its drinks, like the Martinez, date from as far back as the late 1800s. *3713 W. Sahara Ave.; 702-982-8036; herbsandrye.com.*

Parasol Down Dozens of colorful upside-down parasols and a terrace-side lake and waterfall are the draw at this Wynn Las Vegas indoor/outdoor lounge. Mixologist Patricia Richards, who created the Strawberry & Grapefruit Collins (p. 134), is behind the drink list. *3131 Las Vegas Blvd. S.; 702-770-7000; wynnlasvegas.com.*

WEST COAST

SAN DIEGO

Craft & Commerce Philip Ward of New York City's Mayahuel helped with the drink menu at this rustic-industrial Little Italy spot. Don't miss the Mother's Ruin punch for four (gin, spiced black tea, sweet vermouth, citrus juices and Champagne) and beer cocktails like Up in Smoke (barrel-aged Tripel ale, Islay Scotch and apple and lime juices). *675 W. Beech St.; 619-269-2202; craft-commerce.com.*

El Dorado Live music, DJs and bartenders who are obsessed with well-made old-school cocktails define this bar decked out like a Western saloon. *1030 Broadway; 619-237-0550; eldoradobar.com.*

Noble Experiment Sam Ross of New York City's Little Branch consulted on the drink list at this exclusive, gorgeous bar accessed through the burger joint Neighborhood. Entry is only guaranteed by a text message saying, "You're on the list." *777 G St.; 619-888-4713; noble experimentsd.com.*

LOS ANGELES AREA

1886 Bar Cocktail veterans Marcos Tello and Aidan Demarest are behind this charming new retro-appointed bar inside the lovely Raymond Restaurant. Along with the kitchen's grilled octopus, don't miss the Orange Grove, an intense orange-spiked gin-and-tonic. *1250 S. Fair Oaks Ave., Pasadena; 626-441-3136; theraymond.com.*

Copa d'Oro Headed by Vincenzo Marianella, Copa d'Oro has a "be your own mixologist" option. This allows guests to concoct their own drinks with seasonal ingredients (kumquats or sage, for instance) and a choice of top-notch spirits. *217 Broadway, Santa Monica; 310-576-3030; copadoro.com.*

The Edison Andrew Meieran's crew serves handcrafted cocktails, an amazing gin selection and snacks like bacon-maple beer nuts at this lounge inside an old power plant. *108 W. Second St., Los Angeles; 213-613-0000; edisondowntown.com.*

La Descarga
This well-stocked Old Havana–inspired rum bar serves vintage rum cocktails and hosts classes about the spirit in its "cigar room" (an enclosed terrace). *1159 Western Ave., Hollywood; 323-466-1324; ladescargala.com.*

Las Perlas Channeling a colorful barrio fiesta, Las Perlas specializes in mezcal, both neat and in cocktails like El Melón (mezcal, citrus juice, goji berries, cantaloupe foam and edible flowers). *Chicharrónes* (fried pork skins) are among the tasty bar snacks. *107 E. Sixth St., Los Angeles; 213-988-8355; lasperlas.la.*

Musso & Frank Grill
The cocktail and food menus (and the bow-tied waiters) at Hollywood's oldest restaurant have remained virtually unchanged since the place opened in 1919. Actors like Brad Pitt, however, have replaced the old Silver Screen clientele. *6667 Hollywood Blvd., Hollywood; 323-467-7788; mussoandfrankgrill.com.*

Rivera Guests at John Rivera Sedlar's modern Latin restaurant can sample a dozen seasonal tequila infusions (grapefruit-and-star-anise among them), all on tap, as well as Rivera's private-label, extra-aged añejo. *1050 S. Flower St., Los Angeles; 213-749-1460; riverarestaurant.com.*

Roger Room To find this tiny, speakeasy-like bar, look for the neon tarot card signs for the fortune-telling parlor next door.

Dapper bartenders make drinks like the Thug: bourbon, honey liqueur, lemon juice and habanero-infused bitters. *370 N. La Cienega Blvd., West Hollywood; 310-854-1300.*

Seven Grand Part Irish pub, part English hunting lodge, this hip second-floor lounge serves 300 whiskeys and Maker's Mark–dipped cigars. *515 W. Seventh St., Los Angeles; 213-614-0737; sevengrand.la.*

The Tasting Kitchen
At this terrific restaurant, where nearly everything (butchering, pickling, curing) is done in-house, John Coltharp (who contributed the Whiskey chapter on p. 90) and Justin Pike give the same careful attention to the drinks. *1633 Abbot Kinney Blvd., Venice; 310-392-6644; thetastingkitchen.com.*

Tiki-Ti Ray Buhen tended bar at Don the Beachcomber's in the '30s and opened this tiny, Polynesian-themed spot in 1961. His family runs Tiki-Ti now, offering more than 85 tropical drinks. *4427 Sunset Blvd., Hollywood; 323-669-9381; tiki-ti.com.*

The Varnish
A collaboration between cocktail magnates Sasha Petraske and Eric Alperin, The Varnish is accessed through a secret door at Cole's, the destination French Dip restaurant. *118 E. Sixth St., Los Angeles; 213-622-9999; thevarnishbar.com.*

SAN FRANCISCO
15 Romolo Bartenders at this 21st-century saloon whip up intriguing concoctions like the Spaghetti Western: American rye, Italian Campari, organic tomatoes and a splash of pilsner. *15 Romolo Pl.; 415-398-1359; 15romolo.com.*

Absinthe Francophiles crowd the copper-topped tables at this San Francisco institution. The draw: stellar cocktails and brasserie-style dishes from former Michael Mina chef Adam Keough. *398 Hayes St.; 415-551-1590; absinthe.com.*

The Alembic Daniel Hyatt runs the bar at this gastropub. He offers a terrific list of "After-Dinner Libations" like brandies and Scotches and "Daytime" drinks like mint juleps. *1725 Haight St.; 415-666-0822; alembicbar.com.*

Bar Agricole Rhum agricole–lover Thad Vogler, who designed the menus for Beretta and the Slanted Door (and created the Agricole Mule on p. 138), co-owns this airy, rustic-industrial tavern. *355 11th St.; 415-355-9400; baragricole.com.*

Beretta At this upscale pizzeria with a late-night cocktail lounge, Ryan Fitzgerald (author of the Gin chapter, p. 44) serves fantastic drinks like the Dolores Park Swizzle (rum, lime, maraschino, absinthe, bitters). *1199 Valencia St.; 415-695-1199; berettasf.com.*

The Burritt Room Inside the Crescent Hotel, this refurbished historic bar attracts both locals and hotel guests for bar manager Kevin Diedrich's classic and market-fresh cocktails. *417 Stockton; 415-400-0500; crescentsf.com.*

Comstock Saloon Star bartenders Jonny Raglin (whose Wonderlust is on p. 136) and Jeff Hollinger run this 1900s-style bar, where they serve period-appropriate cocktails and snacks like whiskey-cured gravlax on rye toast with dill sour cream. *155 Columbus Ave.; 415-617-0071; comstocksaloon.com.*

214

Elixir H. Joseph Ehrmann creates drinks at this refurbished saloon using house-made mixers, seasonal produce (as in his Celery Cup No. 1 on p. 38) and spirits from Bay Area distillers. *3200 16th St.; 415-552-1633; elixirsf.com.*

Heaven's Dog This modern Chinese restaurant and bar from chef Charles Phan of the Slanted Door offers a dozen or so classically influenced cocktails from mixologist Erik Adkins, including his Cap Haitian Rum & Honey. *1148 Mission St.; 415-863-6008; heavensdog.com.*

Rickhouse The newest place from the owners of Bourbon & Branch, Rickhouse specializes in whiskey and punches (including a gingery Pimm's punch with gin and lemon) that are served with giant blocks of fruit-studded ice. *246 Kearny St.; 415-398-2827; rickhousebar.com.*

The Slanted Door Many of the Slanted Door's drinks—such as Jennifer Colliau's limey Badminton Cooler (p. 162)—are designed to complement chef Charles Phan's modern Vietnamese food. *1 Ferry Bldg.; 415-861-8032; slanteddoor.com.*

Smuggler's Cove Although this bar looks kitschy (tikimania!), mixologist-owner Martin Cate stocks over 200 rums and serves traditional drinks of the Caribbean islands and Prohibition-era Havana. *650 Gough St.; 415-869-1900; smugglerscovesf.com.*

PORTLAND, OR
Beaker & Flask This restaurant and bar from Kevin Ludwig serves inspired cocktails like the Paul Revere (bourbon, bianco vermouth and Pinot Noir grenadine) alongside seasonal dishes such as maple-braised pork belly.

727 SE Washington St.; 503-235-8180; beakerandflask.com.

Central It looks like a humble crêperie, but in a hip, high-ceilinged space behind a black curtain, bartenders shake up concoctions like the Sweetie Pie, a mix of rum, apple cider and allspice liqueur. *220 SW Ankeny; no phone.*

Clyde Common Jeffrey Morgenthaler oversees the rotating cocktail list at this airy "tavern" adjacent to the Ace Hotel. One to try: the Benedict Arnold, with rye, orange pekoe–infused Bénédictine, lemon juice and club soda. *1014 SW Stark St.; 503-228-3333; clydecommon.com.*

Teardrop Cocktail Lounge The bartenders at Teardrop's circular bar make their own tonic water and specialty liqueurs for drinks like the Devil You Know (green Chartreuse, Amaro Nonino, Dolin Blanc vermouth and lime juice shaken with an egg white). *1015 NW Everett St.; 503-445-8109; teardroplounge.com.*

SEATTLE

Liberty This laid-back Capitol Hill spot serves sushi, but it's better known for Andrew Friedman's drinks, among them the Japanese Gardener: Japanese whisky, apricot liqueur, lemon juice and Peychaud's bitters served over a big ball of ice. *517 15th Ave. E.; 206-323-9898; libertybars.com.*

Mistral Kitchen A destination for both its food and its cocktails—like the flaming Bergamot Blazer (overproof bourbon, Earl Grey tea, elderflower syrup and lemon zest)—this sprawling restaurant is also gorgeously modern and spare. *2020 Westlake Ave.; 206-623-1922; mistral-kitchen.com.*

Rob Roy You can order Anu Apte's Ginger Persuasion (p. 32) or Zane Harris's Aster Family Sour (p. 132) at this cool, 1970s-inspired cocktail den. *2332 Second Ave.; 206-956-8423; robroyseattle.com.*

Tavern Law From the duo behind the gastropub Spur, Tavern Law has classic cocktails, lots of whiskeys and fancy bar snacks like oxtail *banh mi* sandwiches. Through a heavy vault door is Needle & Thread, an upstairs bar where drinks are custom-made. *1406 12th Ave.; 206-322-9734; tavernlaw.com.*

Vessel For years, cocktail aesthetes have come to this elegant, modern bar in a renovated 1920s building for swizzles, flips and other drinks, including bartender Jim Romdall's Seersucker Fizz (p. 134). Vessel will move to a new space in summer 2011 (check the website for updates). *vesselseattle.com.*

Zig Zag Café At this restaurant and bar near Pike Place Market, acclaimed bartender Murray Stenson serves forgotten drinks based on old cocktail recipes, like the White Lion: rum, lemon juice, falernum and bitters. Delicious small plates include the Sautéed Calamari on p. 98. *1501 Western Ave.; 206-625-1146; zigzagseattle.com.*

THE FOOD GUIDE

These restaurants and cocktail spots provided some of the delicious, drink-friendly recipes for our Party Food chapter (p. 172).

Animal
435 N. Fairfax Ave.
Los Angeles
323-782-9225
animalrestaurant.com

The Breslin
16 W. 29th St.
Manhattan
212-679-1939
thebreslin.com

B Spot
28699 Chagrin Blvd.
Woodmere, OH
216-292-5567
bspotburgers.com

Craigie on Main
853 Main St.
Cambridge, MA
617-497-5511
craigieonmain.com

Duchamp
2118 N. Damen Ave.
Chicago
773-235-6434
duchamp-chicago.com

Estadio
1520 14th St. NW
Washington, DC
202-319-1404
estadio-dc.com

FishTag
222 W. 79th St.
Manhattan
212-362-7470
fishtagrestaurant.com

Girl & the Goat
809 W. Randolph St.
Chicago
312-492-6262
girlandthegoat.com

The Hurricane Club
360 Park Ave. South
Manhattan
212-951-7111
thehurricaneclub.com

Kith & Kin
1119 W. Webster Ave.
Chicago
773-472-7070
knkchicago.com

The Lazy Goat
170 Riverplace Dr.
Greenville, SC
864-679-5299
thelazygoat.com

Lincoln Restaurant
3808 N. Williams Ave.
Portland, OR
503-288-6200
lincolnpdx.com

Lukshon
3239 Helms Ave.
Culver City, CA
310-202-6808
lukshon.com

Mercat
45 Bond St.
Manhattan
212-529-8600
mercatnyc.com

Second Bar + Kitchen
200 Congress Ave.
Austin
512-827-2750
congressaustin.com

Senate
1212 Vine St.
Cincinnati
513-421-2020
senaterestaurant.com

Shepherd's Pie
18 Central St.
Rockport, ME
207-236-8500

Watts Grocery
1116 Broad St.
Durham, NC
919-416-5040
wattsgrocery.com

BARWARE GUIDE

VODKA

P. 28 "Orsini" votive, conranusa.com; "Roost" highball glass, globaltable.com; tumbler from ABC Carpet & Home, 212-473-3000. **P. 31** "Kaleido" wallpaper, wallpapercollective.com; "Paloma" flutes, crateandbarrel.com. **P. 35** "Fern" Champagne saucer, williamyeowardcrystal.com. **P. 37** "Tifone" tray by Armani/Casa, 212-334-1271; "Bossa Nova" martini glass by Nachtmann, glassware.riedel.com. **P. 41** "Silodesign" highball glass, unicahome.com; "Rolo" shot glass, crateandbarrel.com.

GIN

P. 44 "Harmonie" ice bucket, baccarat.com; "Carat" highball glasses, orrefors.us; "Abysse" wineglass, baccarat.com. **P. 47** "Goldoni" wallpaper, osborneandlittle.com; "Mitos" Cognac glass by Květná, tableartonline.com. **P. 51** "Kikatsu" glass from ABC Carpet & Home, 212-473-3000. **P. 55** "18th Century–Inspired" glass by BollenGlass from John Derian, 212-677-3917. **P. 57** "Essence" wineglass, iittala.com.

TEQUILA

P. 60 "Divine" coupe, orrefors.com; "Caroline" wineglass, williamyeowardcrystal.com.

P. 63 Mode "Darcy" wallpaper by Graham & Brown, target.com; "Hotto" highball glass, orrefors.us. **P. 67** "Coro Gold" highball glass by LSA, conranusa.com. **P. 69** "Patrician" finger bowl by Josef Hoffmann for Lobmeyr, neuegalerie.org. **P. 73** "Pulse" martini glass, calvinklein.com.

RUM

P. 77 "Pythagore" Champagne saucers by J.L. Coquet, devinecorp.net. **P. 79** Ornamenta "Vice Versa" wallpaper, starkcarpet.com; "Bar" double old-fashioned glass, moserusa.com. **P. 83** "Meadow" tumbler, williamyeowardcrystal.com. **P. 85** "Casanova" martini glass, moserusa.com. **P. 89** "Davina" coupe, williamyeowardcrystal.com.

WHISKEY

P. 90 "Kikatsu" glasses from ABC Carpet & Home, 212-473-3000; "Equinoxe" highball glass, baccarat.com; "Hôtel Silver" cocktail shaker from Bergdorf Goodman, 212-753-7300. **P. 93** "Klassisk Rand" wallpaper, countryswedish.com; "Legin" flute, moserusa.com. **P. 97** "88/1 Series" wineglasses by NasonMoretti, seguso.com. **P. 99** "Cubism" glass, moserusa.com. **P. 101** "Verve" cocktail glass, steuben.com.

BRANDY

P. 104 "Culbuto" decanter, moserusa.com; "Juwel" coupe by Theresienthal, tableartonline.com; "Hostess" dish by Kelly Wearstler for Bergdorf Goodman, 212-753-7300. **P. 107** "Ravenna" wallpaper, osborneandlittle.com; "Larabee Dot" martini glass by Kate Spade, Lenox.com. **P. 111** "Abysse" tumbler, baccarat.com. **P. 117** "Monique" glasses by Astier de Villatte from John Derian, 212-677-3917.

PUNCHES

P. 118 "Olivia" tumblers and "Berry" Revere bowl, juliska.com. **P. 121** "Nimbus" wallpaper, fschumacher.com; punch bowl from L. Becker Flowers, 212-439-6001; "Dvorak" tumbler by Armani/Casa, 212-334-1271. **P. 125** "Hotto Cut Lines" cups, orrefors.us.

MIXOLOGIST ALL-STARS

P. 130 Brass dish by Kelly Wearstler for Bergdorf Goodman, 212-753-7300; "Tortoise" highball glass by Ted Muehling, steuben.com; "Cliff" old-fashioned glass by NasonMoretti, seguso.com. **P. 133** "Spherica" wallpaper, fschumacher.com; "Amor Vincit Omnia" Champagne coupe, orrefors.us. **P. 137** "Essence" glass, iittala.com. **P. 141** "TAC 02" highball glass by Rosenthal, unicahome.com. **P. 145** "Square"glass from ABC Carpet & Home, 212-473-3000.

CHEFS' COCKTAILS

P. 148 "Patrician" Champagne coupe by Josef Hoffmann for Lobmeyer, neuegalerie.org; "Hôtel Silver" cocktail shaker from Bergdorf Goodman, 212-753-7300. **P. 151** "Circo di Tivoli" wallpaper, starkcarpet.com; "Lancelot" highball glass, moserusa.com. **P. 155** "Mitos" Champagne coupe by Květná, tableartonline.com. **P. 157** "Frosted Paillette" double old-fashioned glass by Kim Seybert from Barneys New York, 212-826-8900.

MOCKTAILS

P. 159 "Aliseo" flute by NasonMoretti, seguso.com. **P. 161** "Octavio" wallpaper by Mulberry, leejofa.com; "Platinum Paillette" tumblers by Kim Seybert from Barneys New York, 212-826-8900. **P. 165** "18th Century–Inspired" water glass by BollenGlass from John Derian, 212-677-3917. **P. 169** "Herringbone" water glass, calvinklein.com.

PARTY FOOD

P. 172 "Imperial Trellis" wallpaper, fschumacher.com. **P. 177** "Inca" salad plate, daniellevyporcelain.com; gold runner from ABC Carpet & Home, 212-473-3000. **P. 193** "Queen Anne" plate, dbohome.com. **P. 197** "Gold-brushed" ceramic bowl, ochrestore.com. **P. 203** "Hemisphere" plates in gold stripe and Toundra Fall by J.L. Coquet, devinecorp.net.

RECIPE INDEX

★ INDICATES CLASSIC COCKTAILS. PAGE NUMBERS IN **BOLD** INDICATE PHOTOGRAPHS.

RECIPE INDEX

★ INDICATES CLASSIC COCKTAILS. PAGE NUMBERS IN **BOLD** INDICATE PHOTOGRAPHS.

THANK YOU

In addition to everyone who contributed recipes, the following people were indispensable in making this book possible:

Rudy Aguero

Jacques Bezuidenhout

Greg Boehm

Erick Castro

Simon Ford

Ted Kilgore

Vincenzo Marianella

Valerie Meehan

Jaime Reixach

Jalinson Rodriguez

Brian Shebairo

Ross Simon